KEY
WOMEN
WRITERS

EDITOR SUE ROE

SIMONE
DE BEAUVOIR

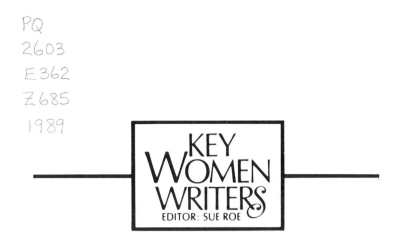

KEY
WOMEN
WRITERS
EDITOR: SUE ROE

SIMONE DE BEAUVOIR

JANE HEATH

HARVESTER WHEATSHEAF

NEW YORK LONDON TORONTO SYDNEY TOKYO

First published 1989 by
Harvester Wheatsheaf,
66 Wood Lane End, Hemel Hempstead,
Hertfordshire, HP2 4RG

A division of
Simon & Schuster International Group

Printed and bound in Great Britain by
Billing and Sons Ltd, Worcester

British Library Cataloguing in Publication Data

Heath, Jane, 1946–
    Simone de Beauvoir – (Key women writers)
    1. Fiction in French. Beauvoir, Simone de.
    Critical studies
    I. Title   II. Series
    843'.912

    ISBN 0–7108–1159–4
    ISBN 0–7108–1161–6

    1 2 3 4 5   93 92 91 90 89

IN MEMORIAM
John Ellerington

Titles in the Key Women Writers Series

Susan Sheridan	*Christina Stead*
Patsy Stoneman	*Elizabeth Gaskell*
Nicole Ward Jouve	*Colette*
Jane Heath	*Simone de Beauvoir*
Rebecca Ferguson	*Alice Walker*
Coral Ann Howells	*Jean Rhys*

Key Women Writers
Series Editor: Sue Roe

The *Key Women Writers* series has developed in a spirit of challenge, exploration and interrogation. Looking again at the work of women writers with established places in the mainstream of the literary tradition, the series asks, in what ways can such writers be regarded as feminist? Does their status as canonical writers ignore the notion that there are ways of writing and thinking which are specific to women? Or is it the case that such writers have integrated within their writing a feminist perspective which so subtly maintains its place that these are writers who have, hitherto, been largely misread?

In answering these questions, each volume in the series is attentive to aspects of composition such as style and voice, as well as to the ideas and issues to emerge out of women's writing practice. For while recent developments in literary and feminist theory have played a significant part in the creation of the series, feminist theory represents no specific methodology, but rather an opportunity to broaden our range of responses to the issues of history, psychology and gender which have always engaged women writers. A new and creative dynamics between a woman critic and her female subject has been made possible by recent developments in feminist theory, and the series seeks to reflect the important critical insights which have emerged out of this new, essentially feminist, style of engagement.

It is not always the case that literary theory can be directly transposed from its sources in other disciplines to the practice of reading writing by women. The series investigates the possibility that a distinction may need to be made between feminist politics and the literary criticism of women's writing which has not, up to now, been sufficiently emphasised. Feminist reading, as well as feminist writing, still needs to be constantly interpreted and re-interpreted. The complexity and range of choices implicit in this procedure are represented throughout the series. As works of criticism, all the volumes in the series represent wide-ranging and creative styles of discourse, seeking at all times to express the particular resonances and perspectives of individual women writers.

Sue Roe

Contents

Acknowledgements

I would like to thank Peter Hulme for being there to supervise my thesis and to discuss the plan for this book. Graham Seymour was kind enough, several years ago, to read and discuss an earlier version of my reading of *Les mandarins* – I am most grateful for his valuable suggestions, and the time he gave so generously. My thanks also to Colette Barbe for her help and advice with the translations from French.

Grateful acknowledgement is made to André Deutsch for UK permission to translate from *Memoirs of a Dutiful Daughter*, translated by James Kirkup, copyright © The World Publishing Company, 1959, *The Prime of Life*, translated by Peter Green, copyright © The World Publishing Company, 1962, *Force of Circumstances*, translated by Richard Howard, © G. P. Putman's Sons, 1974, *All Said and Done*, translated by Patrick O'Brian, copyright © André Deutsch, Weidenfeld & Nicolson and G. P. Putman's Sons, 1974. All reasonable efforts have been made formally to secure copyright permission from the

Simone de Beauvoir

US publisher for *Memoirs of a Dutiful Daughter*, *The Prime of Life*, *Force of Circumstance* and *All Said and Done*, without success. Acknowledgement is however gratefully given. Grateful acknowledgement is made to Jonathan Cape for UK permission and to Alfred A. Knopf for US permission to translate from *The Second Sex*, translated and edited by H. M. Parshley. Grateful acknowledgement is made to Collins for UK permission and to Les Editions Gallimard for US permission to quote from *She Came to Stay*, translated by Yvonne Moyse and Roger Senhouse, and *Les Belles Images*, translated by Patrick O'Brian, copyright © Wm Collins Sons & Co. Ltd, London and Glasgow and G. P. Putman's Sons, New York, 1968; to Collins for UK permission to quote from *The Mandarins*, translated by Leonard M. Friedman, copyright © Wm Collins Sons and Co. Ltd, 1957. All reasonable efforts have been made formally to secure copyright permission from the US publisher of *The Mandarins* but without success. Acknowledgement is however gratefully given.

Notes and abbreviations

It had been my intention to make my own translations of all quotations from the texts studied. For legal reasons this has not been possible in the case of *L'invitée* (*She Came to Stay*), *Les mandarins* (*The Mandarins*) and *Les belles images* (title retained in English). The reader will therefore find footnotes in the text which comment on the published translation. This has been necessary in order to enable me to make certain literary critical points central to my reading.

Translations from texts in French, which are marked with an asterisk in the bibliography, are my own.

After each quotation from texts by Beauvoir, there are two references: the first is to the published English translation and the second is to the French texts (details below).

I have used the following abbreviations:

I *She Came to Stay* (Fontana/Collins, 1979)
 L'invitée (Gallimard, Collection Folio, 1943)

LM   *The Mandarins* (Fontana/Collins, 1979)
      Les mandarins (Gallimard, Collection Folio, 2
      vols, 1954)
MJFR *Memoirs of a Dutiful Daughter* (Penguin Books,
      1963)
      Mémoires d'une jeune fille rangée (Gallimard, Col-
      lection Folio, 1958)
FA   *The Prime of Life* (Penguin Books, 1965)
      La force de l'âge (Gallimard, Collection Folio, 2
      vols, 1960)
FC   *Force of Circumstance* (Penguin Books, 1968)
      La force des choses (Gallimard, Collection Folio, 2
      vols, 1963)
TCF   *All Said and Done* (Penguin Books, 1977)
      Tout compte fait (Gallimard, Collection Folio,
      1972)
CA   *Adieux: A Farewell to Sartre* (Penguin Books,
      1985)
      La cérémonie des adieux suivi de *Entretiens avec
      Jean-Paul Sartre, Août–septembre 1974* (Gallimard,
      1981)
BI   *Les Belles Images* (Fontana/Collins, 1969)
      Les belles images (Gallimard, Collection Folio,
      1966)
DS   *The Second Sex* (Penguin Books, 1972)
      Le deuxième sexe (Gallimard, Collection Idées,
      1949)
E   *Les écrits de Simone de Beauvoir* (Gallimard, 1979)

For excellent summaries of Beauvoir's fictional works,
see Anne Whitmarsh's *Simone de Beauvoir and the Limits
of Commitment* (Cambridge, 1981).

Introduction

Or is it, on the contrary and as avant-garde feminists hope, that having started with the idea of difference, feminism will be able to break free of its belief in Woman, Her power, Her writing, so as to channel this demand for difference into each and every element of the female whole, and, finally, to bring out the singularity of each woman, and beyond this, her multiplicities, her plural languages, beyond the horizon, beyond sight, beyond faith itself?
(Julia Kristeva, 'Women's Time': Kristeva, 1986)

How is it that Simone de Beauvoir produced what is generally agreed to be the most influential analysis of women's condition of this century and yet did not consider herself a feminist until some twenty years later? This question makes certain assumptions about the 'proper' relationship between an author, her texts and her politics, the implication being that theory and practice, the life and the work, should be two sides of the same coin. This notion is crucial within the political

1

domain, since to produce an analysis, to prescribe objectives, a course of action, without demonstrably doing everything in one's own life, in one's own practice, to further them leads to a reduction in personal and theoretical credibility and to dismay among those engaged in the struggle. Many of those who have written about Beauvoir have felt it incumbent upon them to judge her politically, especially in relation to feminism. Was she friend or foe? Was she a misogynist? Just how politically committed was she? Such questions are located in a perceived disjuncture between theory and practice. The obverse of the negative critical response has been the construction of Beauvoir as a powerful, authoritative, knowing figurehead (phallic mother) for the women's movement, which, incidentally, could only be achieved by a process of exclusion – all too familiar to women – of the contradictions in Beauvoir's life and the heterogeneity of her textual production. And so Beauvoir, like 'woman' herself, has been given many identities – sometimes the good, sometimes the bad mother of feminism. Now that she is dead, I detect a reverent attitude which may presage her transatlantic apotheosis.[1]

It is worth noting that for Beauvoir there was no possible contradiction between the theory expounded in *Le deuxième sexe* and her practice. As she explained in an interview in 1984, 'there was nothing polemical about it [*Le deuxième sexe*], it was a very objective, very detached study', but in the early 1970s 'women didn't have much by way of a solid theoretical basis for their beliefs, and so they appropriated *The Second Sex* and used it as a weapon in their struggle' (Wenzel 1986, p. 7). The key word here is 'appropriated'. *Le deuxième sexe* was hijacked, placed in a new (political) context. What must be recognised is that 'Simone de Beauvoir' and/or her

2

texts are constantly being reconstructed to conform with readers' desires. I shall not seek here to construct *my* 'Simone de Beauvoir'. Rather, the focus in this work will be on textuality not personality. But, as a preliminary, I shall refer to the three phases of feminism elaborated by Julia Kristeva in 'Women's Time' in order first to try to locate historically what I see as Beauvoir's (remarkably constant) position in relation to feminism; and second, to lay out my theoretical perspective in relation to the texts studied here. I shall then offer a brief discussion of two aspects of *Le deuxième sexe* by way of example of the approach adopted in the main part of this book.

In Kristeva's first phase,[2] the demand of 'suffragists and existential feminists' is for economic, political and professional equality with men. There is an identification with masculine values and, in particular, women aspire to a place in linear time, in history (Kristeva 1986, pp. 193–5). This encompasses Beauvoir's statement towards the end of *Le deuxième sexe*: 'the "modern" woman accepts masculine values: she prides herself on thinking, taking action, working, creating, on the same terms as males – instead of seeking to run them down, she declares herself their equal' (DS, p. 727: II, p. 485). Kristeva indicates the dangers inherent in this position, pointing out how women who accede to power frequently become 'the most zealous protectors of the established order' (Kristeva, 1986, p. 201). The crucial point is that the oppressive power structure remains intact – it's simply that some women go over to 'the other side'. Beauvoir came to recognise this danger: 'If we put it in class economic terms ... I had become a class collaborationist' (Gerassi, 1976, p. 80). In a later interview with Alice Schwarzer, Beauvoir said 'nowadays feminists refuse to be token women, like I was' (Schwarzer 1984, p. 70).

3

In phase two, post-1968, radical feminists sought to construct a 'simulacrum of the combated society' (Kristeva, 1986, p. 203). This counter-society is structurally identical to the phallic society it seeks to oppose. Kristeva sees this valorisation of the female as a form of inverted sexism. Again, the oppressive power structure is retained, except that now there are two opposing camps, lined up and ready for the 'battle of the sexes'. Because she would have nothing to do with an 'essential femininity', Beauvoir was never implicated in this position. (This explains the hostility towards Beauvoir of those feminists who have adopted this position.) Beauvoir was consistently critical of a separatism founded on a feminine specificity tied to the female anatomy: 'one should not believe that the female body gives one a new vision of the world. That would be ridiculous and absurd. That would mean turning it into a counter-penis' (Schwarzer, p. 79). This is to be contrasted with separatism as a strategic and temporary move in the political fight. Referring to the exclusion of men from women's meetings, Beauvoir rightly pointed out that it is 'a question of the stage reached' (Schwarzer, p. 34).

In the third phase, Kristeva refers to those theories which have called into question the very notion of a stable identity, the corollary of which is that the notion of a fixed sexual identity must suffer the same fate. Kristeva envisages what she calls a 'demassification of the problematic of difference' (Kristeva, 1986, p. 209); in other words, she advocates the dismantling of oppositional power blocs, including masculinity and femininity as entrenched positions. Feminism, Kristeva urges, must break out of phase two, 'belief in Woman, Her power, Her writing' (Kristeva, 1986, p. 208).

When Beauvoir wrote *Le deuxième sexe*, she believed

that socialism would bring with it an end to women's oppression – a conviction she would radically alter. But I wonder whether, beyond the issue of how sexual equality is to be achieved, we may not discern in the dense and often difficult final pages of Le deuxième sexe the adumbrations of Kristeva's utopia. Due, perhaps, to existential philosophy's concern with the individual, can we glimpse, beyond the sexual bipolarity, the outlines of diversity, of differences? Let us be clear, for Beauvoir it is precisely *not* a question of women putting on men's clothes, rather each woman must 'cast off her old skin and cut her *own* new clothes' (DS, p. 734: II, p. 495, emphasis added). Further, in 'a society in which the equality of the sexes was concretely realised, this equality would find new expression in each individual' (DS, p. 735: II, p. 496). Beauvoir goes on to envisage the end of woman as locus of 'feminine charm' (DS, p. 738: II, p. 501).[3] In place of a unified representation of woman (woman as the embodiment of the eternal feminine), there is a change of emphasis to differences, to the singularity of each individual. It is interesting that at this point anatomical difference returns when Beauvoir asserts that a woman's 'relations to her own body, to the male body, to the child, will never be identical to those the male has to his body, to the female body and to the child. Those who talk so much of "equality in difference" could not without ill grace refuse to allow me the possibility of differences in equality' (DS, p. 740: II, p. 503).[4]

It is necessary to say something more about Kristeva's third stage in order to elaborate my theoretical approach to the texts studied here. It is axiomatic to this (psychoanalytic/linguistic) position that sexuality is not pre-given but is produced in language, or more precisely, at the moment (the Oedipus complex) of the subject's insertion into language, the symbolic order. To argue thus is central to what Toril Moi sees as the object of the feminist struggle, which is 'to undo the patriarchal strategy that makes femininity intrinsic to biological femaleness, and at the same time insist on defending women precisely *as* women' (Moi, 1985, p. 82). I take Moi's phrase 'women precisely *as* women' as a political reference to women as a disadvantaged section of society and not as biological females (a reinstatement of intrinsic femininity) (see also below, p. 8).

Consider the following:

1. 'Sexuality is not given in nature but produced' (Heath, 1978, p. 65)
2. 'Sexuality is a fact of discourse which takes into account anatomical determinations' (Leclaire, 1979, p. 44)
3. 'All speaking beings must line themselves up on one side or the other of this division, but anyone can cross over and inscribe themselves on the opposite side from that to which they are anatomically destined' (Rose, 1982, p. 49)

Heath and Leclaire insist on a radical loosening off of the 'anatomy is destiny' equation. (Clearly, anatomy is not to be ignored because it 'figures' in various ways.) Rose points to the precariousness of the process whereby a subject takes on a sexual identity suggesting that there is always the possibility/danger of slippage from one side to the other.[5]

According to Jacques Lacan (see Rose, 1982, p. 46), there is no sexual relation (of woman to man), only each subject's relation to the phallus. In Lacanian psychoanalysis the phallus is the signifier of lack/absence/death. It is that which propels the subject into language

6

(culture) and determines one's relation there. Leclaire reiterates Lacan's insistence that the penis is not the phallus, pointing out that 'because man has in his body a relation with his penis as *the representative of the phallus*' (Leclaire, p. 46), for men, the penis comes readily to 'stand in' for, to represent, the phallus, with the result that man tends *not* to consider himself castrated. It is his fear of the threat of castration that drives him more utterly (than woman) into the symbolic order. He tends to speak the 'discourse of repression' which Leclaire characterises as 'conceptual, philosophical, academic, systematic – a power position' (Leclaire, pp. 43, 47, 52).

Women, on the other hand, tend to have a different relation to the phallus: 'In the whole history and evolution of woman, nothing has ever come as a screen between . . . the phallus, and the way she speaks'; or to put it another way, 'her relation to the phallus is less veiled' (Leclaire, p. 46) Safouan, another psychoanalyst, writes in the same vein of the 'relative ease of women in their relations to the unconscious' (quoted in Heath, 1978, p. 73).

According to Leclaire, these two relations to the phallus give rise to two different types of discourse: 'the repressive' and 'the unconscious or primary type' (Leclaire, p. 47). It would be quite wrong to attribute these discourses to the male and female, respectively. Leclaire is at pains to point out that *they always blend*. He remarks that 'most intellectual women have adopted the universal discourse, the conceptual discourse, the systematic discourse, which is always a discourse of repression' (Leclaire, pp. 46–7). Leclaire speaks also of the need for man 'if he wants to free himself from the prevailing ideological discourse, from a power discourse in which he necessarily participates, he . . . is compelled to call upon *something of the woman in him*'

(Leclaire, p. 45). But, for women, this is treacherous theoretical ground because

> The equation of woman and unconscious leads only to essence; the raising of questions as to the operation of an equation between the feminine and the unconscious as assignment of a place of woman and its complex effects with regard to resistance from that place within a history and economy of repression is a fully political task.
>
> (Heath, 1978, p. 74)

What is suggested in the second part of this quotation is a definition of the feminine not as essence but as eccentric place from which a political struggle (always within language/representation) may be undertaken. The feminine as 'site of resistance to the domination, the definitions, the assignments of the former [the masculine]' (Heath, p. 103).

Another danger. In the present context, given the situation of women in the world today, the sex of a writer *does* matter. What if *Le deuxième sexe* had been written by a man? He would have been speaking for us in a way that Beauvoir, despite many problems, does not. The aversion we have to men speaking for us throws into relief the reality, the urgency of women's political struggle. Post-structuralism has gone beyond an equation of the feminine with biological females and this is liberatory. The problem is that because women, as a group, have so far to go, we cannot yet abandon a (relative) specificity for the feminine as 'women's place'. Overwhelmingly, it is women who have spoken and continue to speak from that place against patriarchy. That men have access to that place may be theoretically accepted but, as male interventions from that place can testify, men, as yet, can speak from it only with unease and discomfort.[6]

My suggestion is that Simone de Beauvoir spoke predominantly the discourse of repression, allowed the man in her to speak. Beauvoir's identification with the masculine has been repeatedly recognised, not least by Beauvoir herself, who did not demur when Alice Schwarzer suggested that she had 'written and created "as a man"' (Schwarzer, 1987, p. 116) In *Histoire du féminisme français*, *Le deuxième sexe* is described as 'cette leçon magistrale' and 'un ouvrage sérieux et scientifique' (Albistur and Armogathe, 1977, pp. 606, 607) – characteristics, surely typical of the power discourse. Margaret Walters wrote of Beauvoir's 'cool, unhesitating authoritative prose' which 'sets up a whole series of absolutely rigid oppositions – masculine vs feminine, culture vs nature, human vs animals, production vs reproduction, activity vs passivity. The first term is always good, the second bad' (Walters, 1976, p. 356).[7] Walters also noted the smooth consistency of Beauvoir's autobiographies, the conscious organisation of the discourse according to a project, and the cost of that consistency in terms of what it excluded (sexuality, dreams, madness). For Walters, this is the limitation of Beauvoir's work for Walters is 'always bothered by a shadow behind the clear outlines of her self-portrait, feelings denied or kept strenuously at bay' (Walters, p. 354).

This recognition of censorship and repression in the texts is the first stage of undertaking a highly productive (if irreverent) reading. Its aim would not be to reproduce textual coherence but to locate the stress points where it seems threatened, most likely to collapse. This, in order to understand the processes at work in the text – in this case, the return of the feminine against and despite the denials of femininity as a problem, of its repression. Beauvoir's texts are fascinating because *she*, to whom the women's movement owes so very much, wrote, initially at least, from the masculine. (What price aversion (to) theory in this case?) That inscription, highly problematic though not without political benefit (see below), on the side of the masculine goes a long way to accounting for the paradox with which I began: that is Beauvoir's lack of identification, particularly in the early years, with women as a group, or indeed of herself *as a woman*. Of course, it might be objected that prior to the 1960s there was no women's movement, no feminist discourse with which to identify. Nevertheless, I find Colette Audry's comment in her portrait of Beauvoir in the early 1930s significant: 'I was amazed to find, in the woman who was later to write *Le deuxième sexe* . . . such a degree of detachment concerning the position in which women were placed' (Audry, 1962, p. 5).

This situation, according to Beauvoir herself, was dramatically altered in the course of her work on *Le deuxième sexe*. In an interview in 1976 she said, 'In researching and writing *The Second Sex* I did come to realize that my privileges were the result of my having abdicated, in some crucial aspects at least, my womanhood' (Gerassi, 1976, p. 80). Her use of 'abdicated' suggests, I think, a sense of loss, the recognition of a price exacted. This remark can be contrasted with the assertions in the autobiographies that femininity never represented a problem for her on a personal level (see Chapter 2). Thus, despite Beauvoir's denials of the effects on her of culturally-produced femininity (which, for me, figures in her famous 'On ne nait pas femme, on le devient' (note the distanced, ungendered third-person pronoun *on*) which might, for her, be glossed 'I wasn't born a woman and have not become one'), a text as massive as *Le deuxième sexe* and the preoccupation with women in her novels insist on the personal (displaced) problem of femininity.

I shall not attempt to produce a reading of *Le deuxième sexe* here. I shall, however, briefly discuss two aspects of that text which are, I would argue, characteristic of the effects of Beauvoir's inscription on the side of the masculine: first, the question of who speaks in *Le deuxième sexe*; and secondly, the violence, the searing negativity, of the attitude towards women writers.

Linguistics, and particularly the work of Emile Benveniste, has made us attentive to the subject positions inscribed in discourse. Psychoanalysis in its rearticulation of Freud with linguistics, offers a theory of (sexual) identity produced in/as a function of language. Feminists are particularly sensitive to who speaks in a discourse. Shoshana Felman raises this issue in her discussion of Luce Irigaray: 'Is she speaking the language of men, or the silence of women? Is she speaking as a woman, or *in place of* the (silent) woman, *for* the woman, *in the name of* the woman? Is it enough to *be* a woman in order to speak *as* a woman?' (Felman, 1975, p. 3). I want to ask these questions in relation to the Introduction of *Le deuxième sexe*.

The Introduction reveals an awareness of the importance of subject positions: 'But how then shall we put the question? And, to begin with, who are we to put it?' (DS, p. 27: I, p. 31–2). Where does the voice come from that can say:

1. They have no past, no history, no religion of their own. (DS, p. 19: I, p. 20)
2. We [women of today] are no longer in the thick of the fight like our elder sisters – by and large we have won the struggle. (DS, p. 27: I, p. 32)

3. Our perspective is that of existentialist ethics. (DS, p. 28: I, p. 34)
4. But if I wish to define myself, I must state first of all, 'I am a woman'. (DS, p. 15: I, p. 14)

The reader here encounters a tangle of subject positions, a confusion of identities. It seems that Beauvoir speaks *of* women (that is, women as 'other', as object (of research) constructed from the masculine (1), *as/with* women (2), as an existentialist philosopher (3), and *as* a woman (4). This confusion is an effect of Beauvoir's situation when she was writing *Le deuxième sexe* (as well as dramatising the fragmentation of the subject in the writing process). Beauvoir's position was clear much later, for example, during her interviews with Alice Schwarzer when she spoke more consistently *as* a woman, using either the first-person singular or plural.

Towards the end of *Le deuxième sexe*, a chapter entitled 'The Independent Woman' charts the vicissitudes of the intellectual woman for whom femininity is antithetical to independence – 'the fact of being active and autonomous is in contradiction with her femininity' (DS, p. 694: II, p. 438). There is, in particular, a discussion of women and writing, surely a subject closest to Beauvoir's heart and about which we might expect to read something optimistic (for women). But, no. We encounter an antagonistic and devastatingly negative assessment of women's literary achievements. We are presented with the image of a straggling and pathetic band of women writers shackled to their negative position with all their energies spent in the effort to break free. For this reason Austen, the Brontë sisters and Eliot, though receiving some praise, are marginalised in favour of the 'great male writers', Dostoevsky, Tolstoy and Stendhal. What is most devastating is that the possibility of women breaking through into the 'human' (i.e. masculine) world seems to be such a futile hope given the enormity of women's disadvantage, 'This [taking the weight of the world upon their shoulders] is what no woman has ever done, what none has ever been *able* to do' (DS, p. 722: II, p. 479). Where, we must ask, is she in this? The account of women and writing is so grudging, aggressive even. Is this a symptom of the cost to Beauvoir (repudiation of 'everything in her that was "different"' (DS, p. 717: II, p. 472), of writing from the masculine? Is this denigration of women a measure of Beauvoir's guilt which must needs be redirected outwards to a castigation of her fellow writers?

As this section of *Le deuxième sexe* makes explicit, for Beauvoir, the precondition for women intervening in and changing the world was escape from the feminine ghetto. Once liberated, she could work alongside man. This view is in contrast with my position, outlined above, in which the challenge to the masculine, to logocentrism, the logic of identity, is predicated on the feminine as a site of resistance to it. According to this view, while women's place (Beauvoir's ghetto) is marginal to the masculine, its strategic importance in the political work ahead is central.

The problematic of this series is the question of how certain women writers gained recognition from the academy, how they became 'great'. Perhaps Beauvoir's access to that pantheon has much to do with the fact that she wrote from the masculine. Further, as Beauvoir herself pointed out, she was an exceptional woman, who, as a 'token' woman, could be accepted: '[men] were prepared to acknowledge in a friendly way a woman who had done as well as they had, because it was so exceptional' (Schwarzer, pp. 36–7). Furthermore, in the 1940s Beauvoir was not known as a feminist, a threat to be marginalised (though this is not to ignore the storm of abuse following the publication of *Le deuxième sexe*), but rather as a philosopher, a member of an élite group of Parisian intellectuals. Might it not be the case that Beauvoir's position at that time was a crucial enabling factor for the production of what is central for feminism in *Le deuxième sexe*? For, as is argued in Introduction I to *New French Feminisms*, what Beauvoir did in *Le deuxième sexe* was radically to alter the terms of the discourse on femininity. From debates on what the 'true' essence of femininity might be, she called into question the whole idea of essence. It is argued that what enabled her to do so was the fact that she did not consider herself a feminist. She stood, therefore, outside the terms in which the debate had hitherto been carried out. An important determinant in this process was the existential philosophy which informs *Le deuxième sexe*. 'Woman' is there described (and not prescribed) as inessential, as other to 'man', the sovereign subject. The challenge is always to the notion of essence (existence as preceding essence). The situation of women described in the text may indeed be bleak but, since nothing is pre-given, there is everything to fight for: 'in order to explain her limitations, it is to woman's situation that we must turn and not to a mysterious essence – the future lies wide open' (DS, p. 723: II, p. 480).

The point of departure for the readings presented here: the proposition (modifiable) of Beauvoir on the side of the masculine and thus the issue of the effects, the cost of that inscription. My focus, then, is not on 'Simone de Beauvoir – Feminist', but on the feminine in her texts, a psychoanalytical (and political) perspective that takes the feminine and the unconscious as politically disturbing in their effects on the status quo. Not the reduction of the texts to the normative paradigm of, for example, the Oedipal scenario (consistently rejected within the texts; consider Anne in *Les mandarins* and Laurence in *Les belles images*) but the fragility, the failing even, of such structuring processes.

Beauvoir produced a great diversity of texts which include essays in philosophy, sociological studies, a play, novels, autobiographies, travelogues, journalism and prefaces. I have chosen to read three of the novels and the autobiographies, for two reasons. First, Beauvoir's claim to 'great writer' status surely depends in large measure on these texts. It is therefore important to examine them first. Secondly, the texts are narratives and fictions (I include the autobiographies in this category). In fiction, there is less emphasis on the 'facts' (whatever they may be) than on the process of the text. It is by attending to how the texts are organised, how they seek to achieve their effects, that I can work through the proposition outlined above.

Faithful in one respect to narrative tradition, the texts are studied in more or less the order of their publication. Thus, no particular significance attaches to the final chapter. The reader will find here neither climax nor post-mortem, but rather I hope, some pleasure and enough stimulation to read productively and to draw her own conclusions.

Notes

1. Introducing her interview with Beauvoir, Hélène V. Wenzel writes of Beauvoir as 'an ageless, luminous presence' (Wenzel, 1984, p. 5) and in the introduction to the whole volume (written after Beauvoir's death):

And I am made to think that a presence such as Simone de Beauvoir's in this twentieth century, does not cease to be a powerful force, even when the living person is no longer with us . . . the written word offers us a more diffuse and timeless presence.
(Wenzel, p. xii)

2. Although Kristeva presents the three phases sequentially, she also sees them coexisting and indeed blending within a single historical moment (see Kristeva, 1986, p. 209).

3. This proposition might be restated in terms of the rejection of the masculine fantasy of 'Woman' as *the* (absolute) difference. In this scheme, 'Man' stands as the positive term and 'Woman' as the negative, as 'not Man'. Thus 'Woman' has no (positive) identity. Her function is to allow 'Man' to define himself against her (Rose, 1982, pp. 47–57).

4. This reminds me of Heath's remark: 'Anatomy is not destiny but neither is it just irrelevant' (Heath, 1984, p. 289).

5. See Jacqueline Rose's 'Introduction – II', in *Feminine Sexuality*, especially pp. 27–9.

6. See Stephen Heath's 'Male Feminism' (1984), the first sentence of which is 'Men's relation to feminism is an impossible one . . . politically.'

7. We now have an understanding of what is at stake in these logocentric pairs, in which the terms are hierarchised. See Hélène Cixous, extract from 'Sorties', in *New French Feminisms* (Marks and de Courtivron, 1981, pp. 90–1).

16

Chapter One

L'invitée: the phallus strikes back

L'invitée, Beauvoir's first published novel, appeared in 1943. Apart from the war which looms towards the end of the text, the events of the narrative are played out in a near-historical and socio-economic vacuum. Despite this, the text is of such complexity and ambiguity that it has generated a diversity of interpretations, from metaphysical novel to psychological thriller, none of which, including the present contribution, reduces or contains it.

The narrative has its origins in the events of Beauvoir and Sartre's lives in the years between 1935 and 1937. Beauvoir, a teacher of philosophy in Rouen, befriended nineteen-year-old Olga Kosakievicz, a boarder at the school. According to Beauvoir's French biographers, Francis and Gontier, Olga was charming, impetuous, explosive and most important of all, exotic. Her father was a Russian aristocrat who had fled to France during the Russian Revolution, her mother was French. Her friends included 'Rumanian refugees, Poles, Jews driven from Central Europe by the Nazis' (Francis et Gontier, 1987, p. 155). Beauvoir took Olga out, built up a relationship with her, and eventually asked Olga's parents for their permission to take responsibility for her education. As a result, Beauvoir installed Olga in the same hotel as herself in Rouen. Sartre, teaching philosophy at Le Havre, and himself something of an exile (from Paris), was going through a difficult period when it seemed that his contemporaries from the École Normale Supérieure were progressing with their literary and political careers. He was morose and experimenting with drugs. In *Les carnets de la drôle de guerre*, he wrote:

> Basically what we were yearning for was a disorderly life ... we needed to go over the top because we'd been moderate for too long. The whole thing came to an end with that black mood which turned to madness just before March that year – and finally, with my meeting O. who was precisely everything we desired and who made us see it quite clearly.
>
> (Sartre, 1983, p. 101)

Sartre, Beauvoir and Olga formed what they called a 'trio', a new and unconventional sort of relationship. According to Beauvoir, the trio was Sartre's invention which grew out of his growing attachment to Olga. This affection grew into a passion of such intensity that the equilibrium of the trio was threatened and finally it broke up. Sartre subsequently 'moved on' to Olga's sister, Tania, who, he wrote in a letter to Beauvoir in 1940, was 'becoming more and more "my child" just like Z [Olga] once was for you' (Sartre, *Lettres*, 1983 Vol. 2, p. 219).

Of course, the 'truth' of the events of those two years is not directly accessible to us, even if, gripped by the biographer's desire, that should be our objective. The events exist in a series of narratives each of which represents them in a different discursive form. With each new version, we receive a fresh set of coordinates that, instead of allowing us to pin down the 'truth', in fact confounds such a project, as 'truth' is endlessly displaced. The value of such narratives lies not in their relation to some original (absent) event but in their transmutational relationships with each other.

In this case, we have *L'invitée*, begun in 1938 and accepted for publication late in 1941. In the second volume of Beauvoir's autobiography, *La force de l'âge* (1960), the story is retold, together with several pages of authorial exegesis concerning *L'invitée*. There are several references to Olga in *Les carnets de la drôle de guerre*. There are letters to Olga and to Beauvoir in Sartre's *Lettres au Castor et à quelques autres*. Finally, there is the Ivich/Mathieu/Marcelle story in Sartre's *L'âge de raison*.

My purpose here is not to attempt to chart the transformations from text to text, nor compliantly to accept Beauvoir's interpretation of *L'invitée*, nor yet is it to engage in a dialogue with her which would seek to oppose my reading to hers. My object is the text itself, its conscious dyadic structure (the Hegelian drama), its insistent exploration and experimentation with triads, the irreducibility of these to a normalised Oedipal scenario and its representation of a disruptive, threatening and dynamic femininity.

The novel begins with an epigraph from Hegel: 'Each conscience pursues the death of the other.' At this conscious level the text offers itself as a Hegelian drama of subjectivity, and indeed the text neatly and quite literally delivers at its end what it had stated at the beginning. It was in terms of the Hegelian struggle that Beauvoir saw her project. Françoise murders Xavière because, as long as Xavière continues to live, her image of Françoise (a Françoise who has betrayed Xavière by sleeping with Gerbert) will continue to exist. So for Françoise, at the end, it comes down to a simple her or me, self or other. In *L'invitée* the struggle is between two women (Pierre is not implicated at this level). The sex of the protagonists and what that means in the context of the Hegelian struggle contrasts with the analysis of women's subordination to men Beauvoir gave some eight years later in *Le deuxième sexe*. Beauvoir argued in that book that a crucial element in that subordination was women's reluctance to take up the Hegelian challenge and indeed their complicity with a process that constructs them as inessential, as object. Anne Whitmarsh, in *Simone de Beauvoir and the Limits of Commitment*, makes a connection between the Hegelian problematic in the two texts. She recognises that 'le regard' (the 'look') 'is particularly menacing for women (both Anne in *Les mandarins* and Françoise in *L'invitée* suffer from it) because the notion of possession joins that of being treated like an object, a notion explicitly treated in *Le deuxième sexe*' (Whitmarsh, 1981, p. 40). However, Whitmarsh does not draw attention to the fact that the struggle in *L'invitée* is between two women. At the beginning of the text Françoise thinks of herself as a sovereign subject. She is masculine in the sense that she likes to *look*: 'I love to look on. I'm fascinated just listening to the music and watching the people' (I, p. 24, p. 38).[1]

The contradiction between *L'invitée*, a text which stages a woman's engagement (to the death) in the Hegelian struggle, and *Le deuxième sexe*, which argues for women's refusal of that engagement, can be read productively. *L'invitée* goes some way (but only some way because there is no encounter between a man and a woman) to calling into question the argument of *Le deuxième sexe*. More radically, *L'invitée* shows a woman taking up a masculine position. This is not to applaud Françoise but to read her case as an example of the loosening off of the connection between the female and femininity, the male and masculinity.

Beyond the two-cornered fight *L'invitée* poses the problem of the eternal triangle. The text has a predominantly triadic structure. Its drama is activated by the intrusion of a third party into a twosome (a dyad). Or to put it another way, two's company and three's a crowd. The reader is actually presented with a series of triangles, with one protagonist featuring in more than one triangle. The principal triad comprises Françoise/Pierre/Xavière, with further triads subtending it: Elisabeth/Claude/Suzanne, Xavière/Gerbert/Pierre, Xavière/Gerbert/Françoise, Elisabeth/Pierre/Françoise. How are we to approach this insistence on the triangle?

My perspective is derived from the account of the construction of the subject (as irremediably split) and of sexual identity (as precarious) proposed by Lacanian psychoanalysis. The locus of these constructions is the Oedipus complex the function of which is to impose a cultural and sexual ordering on the hitherto disorganised child. The process has to do with the child's accession to language (becoming a speaking subject) and with the imposition of a sexual identity which exceeds any natural division, that is, not reducible to biological/anatomical difference.

Any consideration of the Oedipal drama must take account of the dyadic relationship (between mother and child) that precedes it. The paradigm for this dual relationship is to be found in Lacan's mirror phase, which belongs to the Imaginary register and not to the Symbolic. The child sees itself in a mirror (or has its image metaphorically reflected back). This reflected image is unified, coordinated at a time when the child is in a state of motor incoordination. The child identifies with this wonderful (fictional) ideal image. (The lure of this sort of fiction will exist throughout life.) At this stage, the child is locked into a closed two-way circuit in which self and other are interchangeable. The Imaginary is a register in which resemblance operates, a narcissistic relation which is characterised by love and hatred: love when the image is perceived as the self and hatred when it is perceived as a rival. This mirrored 'I' (the domain of the Imaginary) is not yet a social 'I' (the domain of the Symbolic). This will come later when the Law of the father disrupts the mother–child dyad during the Oedipus complex and its dissolution. It is then that the child accepts its positioning in the social formation and becomes a speaking subject.[2]

In the pre-Oedipal situation both the male and the female child form a dyadic relationship with the mother. The normalised outcome of the Oedipus complex requires that the boy renounce his incestuous desire for the mother and identify with the father. The threat of castration propels the boy more powerfully than the girl through the Oedipus complex, because, for him, the penis has been (incorrectly) collapsed into the phallus. He believes he has 'something' to lose. In a sense his penis gets in the way of his relation to the phallus, a situation which does not occur in the case of girls ('her relation to the phallus is less veiled'; see above p. 7).

The progress of the girl child through the Oedipus complex is different. She has to change from a female love object (her mother) to a male one. Fear of castration, the loss of the penis, is of no account to her. It was the difficulty of explaining what drives the girl through the Oedipus complex that caused Freud so much trouble.

According to Jacqueline Rose, it was the problem of femininity and Freud's difficulty in explaining it which comes to reveal the cost of the imposition of the law of sexual difference and its precariousness (Rose, 1982, p. 28).

I have made this detour into psychoanalysis in order to show that the Oedipus complex is now the locus of theoretical attention not because it functions smoothly but precisely for its capacity for malfunction. It has become a 'feminine' strategy to explore its inadequacies, its failures (think of Dora, of whom more later) or even to rewrite the myth of Oedipus (Angela Carter's *The Passion of New Eve*, for example). My argument is that *L'invitée* can be read in the context of this interrogation of Oedipus. Indeed, in its insistence on the triangle it positively invites such a reading.

As a further theoretical preparation for my reading of *L'invitée* I shall refer to Toril Moi's excellent article on 'Jealousy and Sexual Difference' (1982), in which it is argued that women's different relationship to the Oedipus complex and to the Castration complex (i.e. women as pre-Oedipal, that is, less completely oedipalised than men – an extension of the argument about the problem of femininity) is a crucial factor in accounting for the way in which jealousy tends to manifest itself in women. Moi rightly sounds a cautionary note at the end of her article, warning of the necessity of examining the 'changing social and historical contexts' which are an important determining factor in patterns of jealousy. In her conclusion Moi writes:

> Masculine jealousy is predominantly oedipal, and shows a greater frequency of aggressive and paranoid reactions. The jealous man directs his aggression towards the beloved woman, and in extreme cases (*crime passionnel*) he may kill

her. Feminine jealousy is predominantly preoedipal. The jealous woman's reactions are strongly influenced by her ambivalent relationship with the preoedipal mother. . . . If the jealous woman exteriorizes her aggression, she tends to direct it against her rival and not towards her lover.

(Moi, p. 65)

Two recent studies of Beauvoir have sought to use Moi's analysis in order to explain why Françoise murders Xavière in *L'invitée*. Mary Evans finds in the text a 'pattern of traditional sexual jealousy', and she refers the reader to Toril Moi's article (Evans, 1985, p. 132). Judith Okely took as unproblematical the connection between the 'real-life' Beauvoir and the fictional Françoise when she wrote: 'The response of de Beauvoir in real life and of Françoise in the novel, to the threat of a female rival for a man's love follows a standard pattern in jealousy among women which is different from that among men (see Moi, 1982)' (Okely, 1986, p. 137).

These readings construct Françoise as a *typical* jealous woman, and the outcome of the novel as no more than a particularly violent ending to the eternal triangle. There are two points here: first, as I hope to show, a close reading of the text does not justify such a conclusion; and second, we must be careful not to fall into the trap of taking the patterns of masculine and feminine jealousy presented by Moi as normative or prescriptive. The point is not necessarily to map masculine and feminine onto male and female. Moi's article should be seen in the context of the debate on femininity in that it offers further evidence of women's failing relation to the law of sexual difference (in this case, women as pre-Oedipal).

The positions in the main triangle are occupied by

Pierre, Françoise and Xavière. The focus is on Françoise, her subjectivity, with most of the narrative being presented from her point of view. The exceptions are two chapters presented from Elisabeth's viewpoint (Chapter 4, Part 1, and Chapter 1, Part 2) and one chapter from Gerbert's point of view (Chapter 3, Part 2).

While *L'invitée* presents an exploration of triangular relationships, that emphasis on the triangle might be read as the displacement of the problem of the couple. At the beginning of the novel, the relationship between Françoise and Pierre is presented as primary, fixed, established. In a discussion between Pierre and Françoise in Chapter 2, Pierre speaks of his latest affair, which is coming to an end. His womanising does not seem to cause Françoise any distress. Potential difficulties have apparently been resolved by Pierre's considering his relationship with Françoise as in some sense pre-eminent. The words fidelity or infidelity have no meaning for them because, as Pierre puts it, ' '"Toi et moi, on ne fait qu'un"' ' (I, p. 17: p. 29). This key utterance, 'we are as one', appears several times in the early part of the text. In fact, it constitutes a *leitmotif* throughout Beauvoir's literary production, as well as appearing in Sartre's letters to Beauvoir. (We do not yet have her replies.)

What are we to make of this romantic cliché? What is at stake here? Freud noted it when, in 'Civilisation and its Discontents', he wrote, 'Against all the evidence of his senses, a man who is in love declares that "I" and "you" are one' (Freud, 1975, p. 3). Jacques Lacan returned to it in his seminar, *Encore XX*. Jacqueline Rose, discussing 'that fantasised unity of relation', quotes Lacan: '*We are as one. Of course everyone knows that it has never happened for two to make one, but still we are as one.* That's what the idea of love starts out from

. . . the problem then being how on earth there could be love for another' (Rose, 1982, p. 46). The appearance of the romantic cliché seems to be symptomatic of an evasion of intersubjectivity, of confrontation/negotiation with the other. It evokes the interchangeability of self and other, characteristic of Lacan's Imaginary register. What are the features of Françoise's relationship with Pierre? She is dependent on him, 'Nothing that happened was completely real until she had told Pierre about it; it remained poised, motionless and uncertain, in a kind of limbo.' But once she has told Pierre about the moments in her life, they are returned to her 'clear, polished, completed' (I, p. 17: p. 30). Thus Pierre, functioning as a mirror, returns to Françoise a complete (unified?) image that contrasts with the uncertainty (formlessness?) of her impressions.

Even before Xavière's intervention between Françoise and Pierre, Françoise is experiencing the absence of desire: 'She searched for a desire, a regret; but behind her and before her there stretched a radiant and cloudless happiness. . . . No, she could find nothing beyond this abstract regret of having nothing to regret' (I, p. 23: p. 37).[3] This absence of desire is characteristic of a subject caught up in the Imaginary which is a closed system and where there is no desire.

Later, Françoise is in the theatre watching Pierre rehearse his role as Julius Caesar. Pierre is literally an actor on stage, but for Françoise he is also functioning metaphorically as a mirror (see note on pages 44–5). Pierre's body image, his voice and gestures, are reflected back to Françoise almost as if they were her own: 'She anticipated them so exactly that she felt as if they sprang from her own will' (I, p. 43: p. 61). Françoise experiences a nervous excitement which derives from this identification with Pierre and also from a sense of the distance separating her from Pierre, 'And yet, it was outside her, on the stage, that they [the gestures] materialized. It was agonizing. She would feel herself responsible for the slightest failure and she couldn't raise a finger to prevent it' (I, pp. 43–4: p. 61). The text here shows Françoise caught on a knife edge between perceiving Pierre as her double and recognising him as true Other. In the event, Françoise closes off her anxiety by repeating the consolatory cliché, 'we are as one'. However, as the dynamic of the triangle gets under way, Françoise is forced to recognise that the romantic utterance is no more than 'wishful thinking' ('confusion commode').

Xavière functions as a threat to this stultifying, cosy dyadic relation. Unlike the Oedipal drama where the father is the representative of the law of culture which ruptures the mother–child dyad, Xavière stands for Disorder, a challenge to Pierre and Françoise's (masculine) value system. But Xavière's position is more complex than that. The triangle can be read another way: as a staging of the Oedipal drama, a version of the family romance, with Xavière occupying the place of the child, Françoise that of the mother, and with Pierre as father, with all the rivalries and interdictions which that implies.

Let us examine, then, Françoise's relationship with Xavière in the early part of the novel. Xavière does not initially impose herself on Françoise. It is Françoise who befriends her and who subsequently discusses with Pierre how Xavière's future should be mapped out. The English title of the novel, *She Came to Stay*, connotes a 'visitation', an imposition, whereas the French title makes Xavière the one who is invited, Xavière as passive. Xavière thus becomes less an intruder than a victim of the events which follow. She is like a child to

Françoise in the sense that Françoise does choose, albeit ambivalently, to 'have' her.

The language in which Françoise's attitude to Xavière is expressed is that of the coloniser, the metaphor used is territorial: 'what especially delighted her was to have *annexed* this insignificant, pathetic little being into her own life, for, like Gerbert, like Inès, like Canzetti, Xavière now *belonged* to her. Nothing ever gave Françoise such intense joy as this kind of *possession*' (I, p. 11: p. 23, emphasis added). Later, Françoise's attitude towards Xavière is predatory, 'she [Françoise] thought she had acquired a rare treasure' (I, p. 32: p.47).[4]

Xavière, alone with Françoise at the beginning of the novel, is cast in the role of a vulnerable though contrary child. There are repeated references to her face as childlike. But when Pierre is present a different Xavière emerges:

> She smiled and Françoise's uneasiness crystallized. When alone with Françoise, Xavière, despite herself, permitted loathing, pleasure, affection, to be visible on a defenceless face, a child's face. Now she felt herself a woman in front of a man and her features displayed precisely the shade of confidence or reserve she wanted to express.
>
> (I, p. 50: pp. 69–70)

Françoise here confronts the consequences of Xavière's position as daughter which makes her also a rival for Pierre's attention.

The text at times presents Pierre and Françoise as parents. Xavière herself sees them in this role on one occasion – ' "You were like two grown-ups giving a child a good talking-to" ' (I, p. 57: p. 78). One of the rare threads of economic reality is present in the text when Xavière refers to her economic dependence on Pierre and Françoise, ' "I'm accepting your money," she said.

"I'm letting you support me!"' (I, p. 336: p. 416). Pierre
and Françoise's discussion about Xavière's future in
Chapter 2 is conducted in terms that seem almost to
preclude the possibility of Xavière's having anything to
say about her own future: ' "Why don't you bring her to
Paris?" said Pierre. "You could keep an eye on her and
make her work. Let her learn to type and we can easily
find a job for her somewhere"' (I, p. 15: p. 27). So Pierre
and Françoise go about organising Xavière's life to fit
into their world (note that their ambitions for her are
extremely modest). Pierre and Françoise and the milieu
in which they move, the beliefs and certainties which
underpin their lives, represent a pre-existing order into
which Xavière is expected to fit. In the normal process
of socialisation the child comes to accept its insertion
into this pre-existing order and becomes a speaking
subject. Xavière, much to Françoise's indignant surprise,
resists the future that Pierre and she have planned for
her. Her contestatory stance goes so far as to call into
question all that Pierre and Françoise stand for, Xavière's
words 'held a complete set of values that ran counter to
hers' (I, p. 96: p. 123).

In what ways is Xavière a destabilising force under-
mining the status quo, the masculine economy represented by Pierre and Françoise? Xavière is dismissive of
all forms of art which involve the labour of production.
She despises Elisabeth who wants to be a great painter
because she disciplines herself, works to a programme.
Xavière considers that artists, with the exception of
Baudelaire and Rimbaud, are like bureaucrats. Pierre
and Françoise, who is herself working on a novel, are
subsumed in this category of artists or putative artists
who lead tidy, well-regulated lives. Xavière lives in and
for the present. She is contradictory, unpredictable and
resists the judgement of others. She is both literally and

metaphorically disorderly. Her room is a slum. She would happily be a *ratée*, a failure (I, p. 49: p. 69). She seeks and values an unmediated relationship to the world around her. She takes her pleasure neat, or as Françoise remarks, '"You happen to be a little aesthete. You want unadulterated beauty"' (I, p. 96: p. 123).[5] Xavière is not interested in whether music is good or bad, '"I like the notes for themselves; the sound alone is enough for me"' (I, p. 94: p. 121). She has a similar relationship with words: for her they are voluptuous (I, p. 97: pp. 124–5). However, she scorns sitting down at a table and working with them. Françoise sums up Xavière's effect on her when she tells Gerbert that Xavière is a living question mark (I, p. 123: p. 156).

Xavière's interrogatory stance has dramatic consequences for Françoise who begins to recognise words as ambiguous signs: 'when Pierre's words and smiles were directed to her, that was Pierre himself. Suddenly, she felt as if they were ambiguous symbols' (I, pp. 126–7: p. 160). It is as if initially, for Françoise, the signifier (Pierre's words and smiles) had coalesced with the signified (Pierre himself) producing the reassuring certainties of the Imaginary. Now, however, the signifiers have been barred off and Françoise begins to glimpse her alienation as a subject in language. Xavière's function is to force Françoise into a confrontation with herself as split subject. This is achieved, in general terms, by Xavière's attitudes, and in particular through her relationship with Pierre who becomes so involved with Xavière that he can no longer function as Françoise's alter ego. He has to disown 'we are as one', and instead assert that he and Françoise are 'two distinct individuals' (I, p. 57: p. 78). Thus Françoise loses the sense of herself as a sovereign subject, 'Je suis là', 'I am here' (I, p. 1: p. 11) with which the text began. By

Chapter 7 she is completely undermined; she asks the question 'What am I?', and answers, 'I am no one' (I, p. 146: pp. 183–4). Françoise has reached a crisis concerning her subjectivity. Deprived of Pierre as a prop to her (fixed) identity, she seems unable to recognise her radical alienation ('je est un autre') which is a precondition of 'true' intersubjectivity. A similar crisis of subjectivity occurs in *Les mandarins* (see Chapter 3).

My reading of Xavière as a destabilising force in Françoise's orderly life is so far reductive in that I have not emphasised the importance of Xavière as the locus of the feminine within the text, the feminine being defined as that which is problematic to a phallic economy and which always exceeds any attempt at containment. I am arguing that the case of Xavière exceeds both her construction within the text as a rebellious contestatory child and as 'other' with a small 'o', Françoise's adversary in a Hegelian confrontation.

In the second part of the novel, Françoise, Pierre, Xavière and Paule visit a Spanish night club. On the way Françoise calls for Xavière who is staying in the same hotel as Françoise. For Françoise, an atmosphere of evil exoticism and unassuaged desire suffuses Xavière's hotel room, which is described not only as a 'sanctuary where Xavière celebrated her own worship' but a 'hot-house in which flourished a luxuriant and poisonous vegetation; it was the cell of a bedlamite, in which the dank atmosphere adhered to the body' (I, p. 274: p. 342). Note here the emphasis on madness, the body, a different religion (another economy?).

At the night club, there are two women performers. One is a dancer and the other recites a poem. During their performances, Xavière goes into a sort of trance and deliberately burns herself with a cigarette. These feminine performances are characteristic of the Kristevan semiotic. First, a woman, 'plump and mature', elderly even, is completely transformed by her dance (I, pp. 283–4: pp. 353–4). What the text emphasises, and what Xavière watches so intently, is the *movement* of the woman's body. The performance is kinetic, transitory, its product ephemeral. (This compares with Xavière's scorn for works of art, static representations which become objects of exchange.) In the second performance (I, pp. 291–2: pp. 362–3) the text makes it clear that the effect of the poetry has little to do with the meaning of the words, 'Even without full knowledge of the meaning of the words, her impassioned accent, and her face illuminated by emotional fervour were deeply moving' (I, p. 291: p. 363).[6] The audience responds to something (the semiotic) that 'comes through', traverses the words, and which has to do with a quality of the voice, its 'accent passionné', its 'sursauts' (rhythm and movement again), its 'plaintes', a vocal expression of pain, its 'mystérieuses sonorités'.

Let us examine now Xavière's response to the performances and Françoise's reaction to it. During the dance Françoise turns to look at Xavière who 'was pressing the glowing brand against her skin with a bitter smile curling her lips. It was an intimate, solitary smile, like the smile of a half-wit; the voluptuous tortured smile of a woman possessed by secret pleasure. The sight of it was almost unbearable, it concealed something horrible' (I, p. 284: p. 354).[7]

After the performance, Xavière burns herself again:

Behind that maniacal grin, was the threat of a danger more positive than any she had ever imagined. Something was there that hungrily hugged itself, that unquestionably existed on its own account. Approach to it was impossible even in thought. Just as she seemed to be getting near it the

32

thought dissolved. This was no tangible object, but an incessant flux, a never-ending escape, only comprehensible to itself, and for ever occult. Eternally shut out she could only continue to circle round it.

(I, p. 285: pp. 354–5)[8]

Xavière burns herself a third time while the poem is being recited:

Xavière was no longer watching the woman: she was staring into space. A cigarette was alight between her fingers and the glowing end was beginning to touch her flesh without her seeming to be aware of it, she seemed to be in the grip of hysterical ecstasy. . . . This hostile presence, which earlier had betrayed itself in a lunatic's smile, was approaching closer and closer: there was now no way of avoiding its terrifying disclosure. Day after day, minute after minute, Françoise had fled the danger; but the worst had happened, and she had at last come face to face with this insurmountable obstacle which she had sensed behind a shadowy outline, since her earliest childhood. At the back of Xavière's maniacal pleasure, at the back of her hatred and jealousy, the abomination looked, as monstrous and definite as death. Before Françoise's very eyes, and yet apart from her, something existed like a sentence without an appeal: detached, absolute, unalterable, an alien conscience was taking up its position. It was like death, a total negation, an eternal absence, and yet, by a staggering contradiction, this abyss of nothingness could make itself present to itself and make itself fully exist for itself. The entire universe was engulfed in it, and Françoise, for ever excluded from the world, was herself dissolved in this void, of which the infinite contour no word, no image could encompass.

(I, p. 292: pp. 363–4)[9]

Xavière is surely more here than the Hegelian other,

an 'alien consciousness'. Françoise, positioned on the side of a phallic economy, constructs her as a mad-woman, an hysteric. Feminists have already noted the way in which phallocentrism relegates 'woman' as hysteric to the margins. The text, however, effects a reversal which places Xavière at the centre and consigns Françoise to the periphery. 'All you could do was go round it in circles for ever excluded.' Françoise, whose position is similar to that of Lacan when he looks at Bernini's statute of St Theresa, can only gaze in horrified and confused amazement at the 'extase hystérique'. For there is no mistaking the sexual nature of Xavière's pleasure, its excessive *jouissance*. Whatever Xavière stands for, or is, is beyond representation. In the first passage this unrepresentability is conveyed by a metaphor of fluidity – the semiotic again.

There is a slippage from Xavière as 'hostile présence', other with a small 'o', to Xavière in the place of the Other, capital 'O'. In the second passage Xavière as presence is unveiled to reveal absence, a massive lack, death, which no word or image can fill. (This is the crux of the problem for Françoise.) Xavière comes thus to represent the death instinct, a crucial component in the Castration complex.

The following quotation from Laplanche and Leclaire can be read in conjunction with the passage above, in particular, the notions of 'death' ('the death instinct'), 'hysterical ecstasy' ('ecstatic instant', 'a swoon or ecstacy'), 'that no word or image could circumscribe' ('screaming out its appeal for a word'), 'dévoilement' ('to veil and sustain it'):

> The death instinct is that radical force which surfaces in the catastrophic or ecstatic instant when the organic coherence of the body appears as though unnamed and unnameable,

a swoon or ecstacy, screaming out its appeal for a word to veil and sustain it. It constitutes the basis of the castration complex and allows the development of language, together with the possibility of desire and the development of the sexual instincts.

(quoted in Leclaire, 1979, p. 167)

With Xavière, the text stages a representation of the moment/possibility of desire and Françoise's traumatised reaction to it.

I suggested earlier that the text, at one level, inscribes Pierre, Françoise and Xavière in a familial/Oedipal triangle with its attendant loves, prohibitions and rivalries. This triangle can be mapped onto another one that is free of familial interdictions. It is on the text as a version of the 'eternal triangle' that the recent interpretations I referred to earlier have depended. In this scheme Françoise has been seen as the typical jealous heterosexual woman who directs her murderous aggressivity against her rival, Xavière, rather than against her beloved, Pierre. Lest there be any doubt about the inappropriateness of such an interpretation, the text proposes just such a banal eternal triangle in the case of Elisabeth/Claude/Suzanne which functions as a counterpoint to Pierre/Françoise/Xavière. The text does make a connection between this sort of heterosexual jealousy and murder. Elisabeth recounts the violent attack of Moreau, a man who would like to be her lover: '"Just imagine, he pinned me against a lamp-post, grabbed me by the throat, while he shouted dramatically: 'I'll have you Elisabeth, or I'll kill you'."' (I, p. 222, p. 281).

My argument is twofold. First, that the text exceeds the possibility of containment within the familial; and second, that we do have another triangle (but *not* a

35

banal 'eternal triangle') the nature of which I shall try to trace. What is important here is the textual ambivalence, the way in which the familial/Oedipal can be invoked and exceeded. The text seems to evade any attempt to pin it down to one scenario or the other, such is its irreducibility.

Where are the Oedipal interdictions? They arise first in the case of Françoise who has 'a maternal feeling towards Gerbert – maternal with a faintly incestuous touch' (I, p. 36, pp. 51–2). When Xavière is going through a moment of deep depression, Pierre turns to Françoise and angrily asks her to calm Xavière:

> 'You ought to have put your arms around her a long time ago and said – said something to her,' he added lamely.
> Mentally, Pierre enfolded Xavière in his arms and rocked her soothingly, but respect, decency, and strict convention paralysed them, his warm compassion could be embodied only in Françoise.
>
> (I, p. 103: p. 132)

Pierre here is cast in the paternal role in the same way that Françoise is cast in a maternal role in relation to Gerbert. Note also the way in which physical tenderness between Françoise and Xavière as mother and daughter is here legitimated.

As Pierre's attachment to Xavière grows stronger so his role as putative lover develops. The text maintains a delicate equilibrium (ambivalence?) between the roles of father and lover, 'Their relationship was virtually chaste, and yet, through a few kisses and light caresses, he had established between them a sensual understanding, which was clearly visible beneath their reserve' (I, p. 238: p. 299). It seems that Pierre's transition from the role of father to that of lover can be accomplished with relative ease. This must have to do with the fact that the relationship is in both cases heterosexual. The same can be said for Françoise and Gerbert whose relation to Pierre and Françoise is similar to that of Xavière. Both are like children to Pierre and Françoise. Françoise can make love with Gerbert because that too is a heterosexual relationship. However, in the case of Françoise and Xavière, the relationship is homosexual and, though physical contact between mother and daughter is socially acceptable, Xavière as a love-object for Françoise is not.

It remains now to examine that relationship.

Just as Pierre initially plays father to Xavière, so Françoise plays mother. That relationship plays out a mother/daughter rivalry for the father so that, for example, Françoise is shocked to see Xavière's coquettishness towards Pierre. Pierre's increasing involvement with Xavière is presented first of all as a potential threat to the 'we are as one' mythical couple. Indeed the reality of this threat and the structural impossibility of the trio as some new sort of sustainable interpersonal relationship is made evident when Pierre says ' "When I look at her I don't look at you" ' (I, p. 164: p. 206). In other words, he can't look two ways at once. The first effect of Pierre's involvement is a split in the 'unity' of the couple involving an outflow of content, 'Pierre still repeated: "We are but one," but now she had discovered that he lived for himself. Without losing its perfect form their love, their life was slowly losing its substance' (I, p. 154: p. 194).

This rupture produces Françoise's crisis of subjectivity and her flight into illness. By the end of Part I, Pierre, in Xavière's presence, has declared to Françoise that he and Xavière love each other. Pierre's passion has been increased by his fear that Xavière might be in love with Gerbert. This masculine rivalry urges Pierre on so that his earlier reluctance to make physical contact with Xavière evaporates:

'When I said the word "love", she trembled a little, but her face gave immediate consent. I took her home.'

. . .

'When I was about to leave her, I took her in my arms and she held her lips up to me. It was a completely chaste kiss, but there was so much tenderness in her gesture.'

(I, p. 207: p. 258)

This is another example of the text sustaining both the purity (observing Oedipal interdictions) and the sensuality (defying them) of Pierre's relationship with Xavière.

It is at this mid-point in the text that Françoise, if she is to be read as the archetypal jealous woman, will manifest that jealousy. Before examining the text closely, it should be noted that the text has made it clear that Pierre has had a series of affairs (comparisons can be made with Sartre here) but that none of these seems to have caused Françoise any anguish. The reader must therefore ask what is special about Xavière. After all, on several occasions Pierre offers to end his relationship with Xavière. At a banal level, Françoise is never in danger of 'losing' him.

When Pierre declares that he and Xavière love each other, Françoise is deeply upset because of the threat he poses to Françoise's relationship with Xavière. 'She [Françoise] was not jealous of him, but not without a fight would she lose this little sleek, golden girl whom she had adopted one chilly morning' (I, p. 201: p. 252). Later, when Pierre and Françoise are alone, Pierre recounts the end of his successful evening with Xavière and again we have Françoise's reactions: 'The picture seared Françoise like a burn. Xavière – her black suit, her plaid blouse and her white neck; Xavière – supple and warm in Pierre's arms, her eyes half closed, her mouth proffered. Never would she see that face' (I, p. 207: p. 258). This is a textual reversal. Previously it was Pierre who was prohibited from physical contact and who now enjoys it, the interdiction has fallen on Françoise, 'She would never see that face.' Françoise's disarray is compounded by the thought that 'Pierre, with his caressing masculine hands, would turn this black pearl, this austere angel, into a rapturous woman'. And further, Françoise adds, '"It always seems a sacrilege to me . . . to think of Xavière as a sexual woman"' (I, p. 208: p. 260). Is this the jealousy of the mother who recognises but would seek to deny the sexual maturity of her daughter? Or does it indicate another difficulty – that of Xavière as a desiring woman with whom Françoise could have a sexual relationship?

Pierre's visit to Françoise (who is in hospital) is followed by one from Xavière. In a moment of sublime textual ambiguity Françoise looks at Xavière, the woman Pierre loves, 'avec des yeux d'amoureuse' (I, p. 210: p. 263). The ambiguity turns on the word 'amoureuse' – Françoise in love, but with whom? Pierre tries to reassure Françoise that Xavière loves her as much as him. And yet, for Françoise, her relationship with Xavière is submerged, devalued by Xavière's (heterosexual) relationship with Pierre who 'deliberately behaved as if this feminine relationship seemed un-important to him' (I, p. 238: p. 300).

Later, when Françoise is well again, she goes walking with Xavière in Paris. Xavière takes the initiative, making a point of taking Françoise's arm in hers. As they enter a 'bal colonial', a sort of night-club, they see a group of friends, 'she [Xavière] had not let go of Françoise's arm, for she did not dislike having people take them for a couple when they entered a place: it was the kind of provocation that gave her amusement'

(I, pp. 245–6: p. 309). The two women dance, Xavière authoritatively taking Françoise in her arms:

> She felt Xavière's beautiful warm breasts against her, she inhaled her sweet breath. Was this desire? But what did she desire? Her lips against hers? Her body surrendered in her arms? She could think of nothing. It was only a confused need to keep for ever this lover's face turned towards hers, and to be able to say with passion: 'She is mine.'
>
> (I, p. 246: p. 310)

Françoise adopts a masculine, possessive attitude towards Xavière, displaying the features of 'amour captatif' described by Toril Moi in her article on jealousy and sexual difference. The characteristics of this type of love, which Moi takes from the work of Daniel Lagache, are a desire 'to possess the object totally and exclusively', the 'loved object is seen as a thing; not as an independent consciousness: the possessive lover refuses to acknowledge the alterity of the Other, of the beloved.' Moi goes on, 'For Lagache, jealousy can only exist within the limits of the *amour captatif*, and therefore the death of the beloved is the extreme but logical outcome of this kind of love' (Moi, 1982, p. 64). The implication is that this type of love is typically masculine.

Françoise and Xavière leave the night-club, and as they get into a taxi, Françoise feels convinced that she has 'repossessed' Xavière. Back at their hotel, Françoise goes into Xavière's room. But her composure is threatened, she is unable to act, 'paralysed by the frightening grace of this beautiful body that she could not even desire, Françoise was at a loss for a gesture' (I, p. 251: pp. 315–16).[10] Awkward moments follow and just as she is about to leave, Françoise takes Xavière in her arms, 'Xavière yielded, and for a moment she was light

40

and taut against her shoulder. What was she waiting for?' (I, p. 251: p. 316).[11] But Françoise cannot handle her desire. At the very moment she becomes aware of it, it is blocked by a mental and physical paralysis.

The case of Gerbert and his relationship with Françoise provides further evidence of Françoise's masculinity and, to a certain extent, places a question mark over Gerbert's own sexual identity. I have already pointed out that Gerbert occupies a structurally homologous position to that of Xavière in relation to Pierre and Françoise – another Oedipal triangle. At the beginning of the narrative Gerbert is not only childlike for Françoise he is also feminised, with his long girlish eyelashes and his childlike eyelids (I, p. 8: p. 20). In Part II, Chapter 3, written from Gerbert's point of view, we learn that he finds women boring, 'if he had had the good fortune to be a homosexual, he would have associated only with men' (I, p. 269: p. 337). Towards the end of the novel, when Gerbert and Françoise are on a walking holiday, he declares that he will never love a woman (I, p. 366: p. 451). he repeats his distaste for the company of women, a category from which, significantly, Françoise is excluded. ' "You're like a man!" ' he tells her (I, p. 366: p. 452). Françoise finds herself in some difficulty at this stage. She wants to sleep with Gerbert but given the air of masculine cameraderie that has been established between them (' "I know you think of me as a man," ' says Françoise (I, p. 372: p. 459)), she is unable to deploy what she considers to be feminine strategies. There are other impediments. The text emphasises Gerbert's respect (filial love?) for Pierre. 'He was thinking of Pierre. He was thinking that it was impossible to be fonder of anyone than he was of Pierre' (I, pp. 367–8: p. 453). Gerbert hesitates also because he does not want to occupy the same position in Françoise's life as that of the 'other women' in Pierre's life. Gerbert here places himself in a feminine position in relation to Françoise – *he* does not want to be *her* 'bit on the side'. Eventually all these difficulties are overcome and Françoise and Gerbert do make love. It is notable however that in order to do so they have to leave the city for the hills, a natural rather than a man-made (cultural) environment.

If we read *L'invitée* as a family romance, the text stages the Oedipal scenario in its positive (heterosexual) form: the son (Gerbert) sleeps with the mother (Françoise), and the father (Pierre) comes close to sleeping with the daughter (Xavière). While this scenario breaks the incest taboo, the heterosexual injunction remains intact. Thus what remains as a stumbling-block, unresolved, is the question of female homosexuality, the Oedipus complex in its negative form, love for the parent of the same sex (in this case, between mother and daughter). That relationship is present in the form of an absence when Françoise considers the trio: 'She looked at Xavière, then at Pierre – she loved them, they loved each other, they loved her' (I, p. 229: p. 289). What is missing here is that Françoise and Xavière loved each other.

Pierre and Françoise are inscribed within the phallic economy. They are both masculine. The fantasy of unity, the 'we are as one', that initially characterises their arid liaison belongs within the Imaginary. It is a fiction which is shown, ultimately, as just that. Pierre's 'Don Juanism' is a symptom of his entrapment in the Imaginary as he goes from conquest to conquest in his search for the self in the other (see Wilden, 1981, p. 165). But the drama centres on Françoise. She is problematically inscribed on the side of the masculine because, as a woman who desires another woman, she faces an interdiction on homosexuality. (A similar interdiction fell on Dora in Freud's case-history, 'Dora'.) The Hegelian problematic, Françoise's 'either/or', 'her or me' oppositional attitude towards Xavière, is both phallocentric and Imaginary. Within that problematic, Xavière's murder is a dead end since the text proposes no transcendence of the oppositional relation. As Anthony Wilden puts it:

> If one interprets the Imaginary relationship as a Hegelian struggle for recognition, as Lacan does, then one understands that the 'struggle for pure prestige' in the Imaginary cannot depend on any kind of real death. It is in effect dependent on an implicit or unconscious pact between the participants: that they shall both survive, for one cannot be recognized alone. The dialectic must depend therefore on IMAGINED DEATH.
>
> (Wilden, 1980, pp. 468–9)

The radical and political importance of the text is that in Xavière, it represents a dynamic and subversive femininity which exceeds all masculine efforts at containment and control. It is so threatening that it must, ultimately, be eradicated, killed off. It is thus no accident that the first title of the novel was 'Légitime défense', suggesting that Xavière's murder was the justifiable and legitimate act of the forces of law and order – a fatal phallic backlash.

Notes

1. The (published) translation here does not register Françoise's *preference*: she would rather look than listen.
2. Since the concepts of the Imaginary and the Symbolic recur throughout this study, I have tried, at the risk of crude simplification, to offer some notes which may help the reader.

The Imaginary, as the name suggests, is concerned with ideal and therefore pleasurable images of the self. Such images are not a true reflection of the self, they are fictive. This means that in our relations with other people we may see only what we want to see, i.e. *resemblance*. For example, I might say, in relation to another person 'Yes, that's me. I'm like that!' This is also the domain of the double, the *doppelgänger*. Something similar occurs in the case of advertising images. I may identify with a flattering representation and, as a consequence, buy the perfume, clothes, newspaper or whatever, presented as integral to the image.

In the Symbolic, the two-way short-circuit between self and other is broken. In the Symbolic, I have to recognise that other people are different and that in my relations with them I am in some way divided from myself, certainly *not* together!, positioned 'out there' in a variety of ways (as 'she', 'you', part of 'we', or 'they'). It is because of this split that I have to say that as far as intersubjectivity is concerned, 'I am not myself – I am another'.

The following notes relate more closely to Lacanian psychoanalysis:

The mirror phase (the Imaginary register) opens up a first and *necessary* division between self and other. It is an enclosed, two-way *immediate* relation which involves a blurring or merging of self and other. (An example of this would be the situation in which child (a) on seeing child (b) being hit would state that it is she/he, child (a), that is being struck.)

The Symbolic is a three-way, *mediated* relation. During Oedipus and its resolution, the dual relation of the Imaginary is broken by the intervention of a third term, the Law of the father (threat of castration/absence/loss/death). Entry into the Symbolic order, into language, involves the loss of Imaginary plenitude (of the 'Yes, that's me, together, all there!' variety). I am not fully present in language, I am only represented there. The subject as split is dramatised in the utterance 'I am lying'. At first, there seems to be a single homogeneous subject present. However, on closer examination we realise that there must be two subjects, two 'I's: one of which is lying and one of which is not. (The terms used to designate these two 'I's are the 'I' of the statement ('énoncé') and the 'I' of the utterance (énonciation). For further explanation see Heath, in Barthes, 1977, pp. 8–9.) Finally, it is at the moment of entry into the Symbolic, out of that necessary splitting, that the unconscious and desire (for lost Imaginary plenitude) are produced. There is no desire in the Imaginary.

For further elaboration of these points see the chapter on psychoanalysis in Eagleton (1983) and Belsey (1980, Chapters 3 and 4).

3. The published translation fails to convey the aridity of Françoise's happiness. The original text uses the word 'arid'.

4. The published translation fails to convey the violence of Françoise's appropriation of Xavière. 'Booty' would be more accurate than 'treasure' and 'got her hands on' would be better than 'acquired'.

5. The published translation gives 'unadulterated' for the French 'cru': 'raw' would be preferable as it is closer to the French and not value-laden.

6. The published translation is weak here: the original text insists on the fact that the *effect* of the performance is totally independent of an understanding of the meaning of words. Further, the original speaks of a 'visceral' reaction to the performance (i.e. of the body) rather than its being just 'deeply moving'.

7. 'Half-wit' (so pejorative) should be translated 'madwoman' (we know something of *her* history).

8. The published translation does not adequately represent the words of the original, that suggest fluidity. I cannot see any justification for the use of 'occult' in the penultimate sentence. The French uses 'impénétrable' which is of course the same in English. This is important for surely impenetrability is a feminine/feminist response.

9. For the same reason as that given above, 'madwoman' would be preferable to 'lunatic' (line 6). The translation gives 'pleasure' for the original 'jouissance', which is surely to diminish Xavière's experience.

10. 'could not' does not convey the force of 'ne savait même pas' which suggests that Françoise *did not know how to* proceed.

11. 'Taut' is incorrect. The original word is 'souple' which suggests pliancy. Also the French has 'immobile', 'motionless', where the published translation has 'light'.

Chapter Two

The autobiographies: telling 'The Beauvoir Story'

Proposition one: time is a man, space is a woman.
(Angela Carter, *The Passion of New Eve*)

So, she thought, could she at last put circles round her life.
(Vita Sackville West, *All Passion Spent*)

We can never rediscover our childhood, nor the yesterday which seems so near, nor the instant which has just melted away.
(Emile Benveniste, *Diogène*)

Beauvoir's aim, the reader is repeatedly told throughout the autobiographies, is to 'unveil reality' (MJFR, p. 114: p. 158), 'to find the truth and to speak it' (MJFR, p. 345: p. 481), 'to dispel mystification' (TCF, p. 499: p. 633). It is paradoxical, therefore, that this intention to 'tell it how it was' should have resulted in mystification, for that is how Julia Kristeva saw *La cérémonie des adieux*, an account of Sartre's last ten years. 'One must surely be endowed with the naive cruelty of this exceptional

47

woman to create such a myth. . . . I am convinced that she has still not been properly evaluated as a chronicler who knew how to construct an entire cultural phenomenon' (Kristeva, 1984, p. 261). The process of constructing that 'cultural phenomenon' has been largely achieved through Beauvoir's autobiographical project. It may be no accident that the name Beauvoir means 'seeing it beautiful' (though again it could also connote 'seeing in vain' – a confounding of the scopic) for in some ways the autobiographies do give us a 'rosy picture'. The success of the process was confirmed in the obituary notices following Beauvoir's death in April 1986, many of which recognised Beauvoir and Sartre as *the* legendary couple of the twentieth century. The newspaper *Libération* had the succinct and witty headline 'Sartre–Beauvoir': the mythical couple against the myth of the couple' (*Libération*, 15 April 1986, p. 10).

In 1956, Beauvoir, a literary Scheherazade, began a narrative production which, over the following twenty-three years, would amount to five volumes of memoirs, some 2500 pages of print. This textual prolixity, underwritten by apparently exhaustive documentation, amounts to a verbal bombardment which has tended to carry all counter-claims to truth before it. Of course, voices of protest have been raised about inaccuracies (see for example François Bondy, 1965, p. 85). However, such protests have had little effect on the authority of the texts (Beauvoir as 'witness', as in the title of the recent Yale French Studies devoted to her) so that they continue to be viewed as a rich source of historical background material.

We await a critical biography of Beauvoir. In 1985, a biography by Claude Francis and Fernande Gontier was published in French (the English version appeared in 1987). This text is largely complicit with the Beauvoirian project. It embellishes the notion of Sartre and Beauvoir as the legendary couple – the title of the English version is 'A Life . . . A Love Story'. In the preface, Sartre and Beauvoir are constructed as Tristan and Isolde, timeless and romantic lovers. Our fascination with them, it is suggested, has to do with the fact that 'they were a couple and they had this wonderful thing beyond philosophy and the vagaries of politics – total harmony between two human beings' (Francis and Gontier, 1985, p. 12).

Biographies can, of course, be useful and informative supplements to autobiography. In the case of Francis and Gontier, we learn that Pradelle, the young student with whom Zaza falls disastrously in love in *Memoires d'une jeune fille rangée*, was the philosopher Merleau-Ponty, an unacceptable match on account of his being illegitimate (Francis and Gontier, pp. 96–101). The stance of these biographers is collaborative. It joins that of the collusive reader who aims for a completed narrative with no loose ends, or as Beauvoir put it in relation to her autobiography, 'My concern now is to recover my life, to revive forgotten memories, to reread, see again, complete unfinished studies, fill in the gaps, throw light on obscure points, gather things together' (TCF, p. 50: p. 60).

I want to suggest a different way of reading, that of the 'suspicious' reader, who recognises that the narrative is a web of words, an artefact shaped in conformity with a project and that close examination will reveal some of the secrets of its manufacture. This is how I shall approach Beauvoir's memoirs in an attempt to demystify the 'cultural phenomenon'. I shall briefly examine auto-biography as a genre since, as conventionally received, it offers a literary haven to the notion of a coherent unified subject and a fertile space for myth-making. Then I shall examine the discursive organisation of the

49

texts with a focus on two narrative modes. The first, which I shall call the main narrative, ostensibly presents a sequence of events, a linear determinism in which the past acts on and produces the present. The second mode, the meta-narrative, works the other way round: it retrospectively organises events in conformity with a project. This is the process known as *Nachträglichkeit* in psychoanalysis. It suggests that, perhaps, we need to read the history of the person backwards, taking the beginning of the main narrative as an end-point of the structuring processes that have produced it.

One aspect of this process is the way in which the text presents the reader with a set of propositions or meanings in relation to the 'life'. In Beauvoir's case, there is the idea that by the time she left home in 1929 she had 'liquidated' her bourgeois past, that femininity was never problematic at a personal level, and that her relationship with Sartre was an unqualified success. An understanding of the form and context in which such propositions are made and worked out in the narrative is frequently sufficient to undermine their authority, to demystify them.

To write one's memoirs or autobiography is a gesture of strength. As women have come to realise, this is true on both an individual and collective level. It means having a voice, a position, even if, problematically, the condition of this is subjection to the Symbolic order, the question always being how the masculine economy can be changed when collusion with it seems to be a condition for speaking, intervening in the first place. These are not consciously problems for Beauvoir, who did not write *as a woman*. She wrote and spoke the discourse of mastery, and this must surely be a factor in her being recognised as a 'great writer'. The 'cultural phenomenon' to which Kristeva referred is an effect of this mastery so that a deconstruction of the former will imply some disruption of the latter.

Literary theorists have accepted that autobiography and novel are indistinguishable at the level of the text. The novel can deploy any of the textual features generally associated with autobiography. The only way in which autobiography can be generically stabilised (women must always be wary when genre gender is an issue) is by a process of framing, of contextualisation which is a matter of convention, and therefore optional. Linguistics is informative here. According to Benveniste, 'I' and the other personal pronouns are shifters which

> do not refer to a concept or an individual . . . I refers to the act of individual discourse in which it is pronounced, and by this it designates the speaker. It is a term that cannot be identified except in what we have called elsewhere an instance of discourse and that has only a momentary reference.
>
> (Benveniste, 1971, p. 226)

In the case of the written 'I', the writer is absent and the shifter remains radically empty unless the receiver of the text, encouraged by the author, chooses to fill it. The autobiographer seeks a privilege from the reader when she or he asks that, for the duration of the narrative, the 'I' should refer to her or him.

While autobiography raises important issues concerning the author and the subject, it is concerned also with narrative construction and, associated with this, chronicity. My argument is that Beauvoir's autobiographies deploy more than one chronology. In order to throw some light on this matter, I shall refer once more to Benveniste and to his distinction between historical narration and discourse, and to his analysis of chronicity

(Benveniste, 1966, pp. 1–12). Benveniste defines historical narration as a mode of utterance that excludes 'every "autobiographical" linguistic form . . . *je* or *tu* or *maintenant*' (Benveniste, 1971, p. 206). Pure (sustained) historical utterance would seem to be an impossible mode for autobiography since it excludes the subjective.

As for chronicity, Benveniste defines chronic time as the time of events which are situated precisely on a fixed scale, a calendar for example. This is objective time. It depends on an initiating and fixed 'axial moment' (the birth of Christ, for example). It is presumably to this objective time that the producer of historical narration would refer.

Then there is linguistic time which, like subjectivity, is a function of discourse. In this case, the axial moment is the present of discourse, the 'now' of the utterance, with past and future located as points behind or ahead of that 'now'. Linguistic time may, within certain limits, be independent of chronic time (this being guaranteed by the presence of speaker and addressee). But in the case of the written text (no speaker) the utterance has to be explicitly linked into chronic time – this in the interests of intelligibility. The problem is similar to the one mentioned above where the 'I' of discourse, when spoken, obviously refers to the person who uttered it. But when the 'I' is written down it becomes an empty sign which, in order to become meaningful, requires a reference of the 'I' 'so and so' variety.

It is now possible to recognise some of the problems which arise for the putative autobiographer and her reader. The crucial point is that in order to represent subjectivity, the apparatus of discourse must be used which will have at least an implicit reference to the 'now' of utterance but which will also make explicit reference to chronic time for the sake of intelligibility.

This double chronology will produce a narrative tension with prominence being given either to the 'now' of discourse or to chronic time.

This tension is an aspect of the splitting which opens up the gap between the 'I' of the *énonciation* and the 'I' of the *énoncé* (see note on pages 44–5). Just as subjectivity is ephemeral, a function of the instance of discourse, unless by convention the subject is named, so also with time which, according to Benveniste, has only a limited temporal reference forward or back, unless it is connected into chronic time (itself also the product of law and convention).

According to Kristeva, the Symbolic order is a temporal order. Access to and intervention within the temporal order of history and politics is through identification with the father. However, she suggests that in the case of a woman something may escape that identification. That 'something' which Kristeva calls 'time's "truth"', that is, the unconscious which is outside time may produce a marginal discourse which breaks against linear phallic time. She adumbrates what she calls 'an impossible dialectic', that is 'a constant alternation between time and its "truth", identity and its loss, history and that which produces it' (Kristeva, 1986, p. 156). Beauvoir's identification with the father, her access to political and cultural life, is beyond dispute. But perhaps there might be a discourse in her memoirs whose relationship to chronic time would be problematic, which would resist being situated within it. It would surely be a discourse in which the 'now' of utterance with its limited chronological reference (equivalent to the ephemeral nature of the subject in language) would be manifest but not anchored, just as a subject might speak (for a moment) without being named.

Simone de Beauvoir

Beauvoir's five volumes of autobiography, *Mémoires d'une jeune fille rangée* (1958), *La force de l'âge* (1960), *La force des choses* (1963), *Tout compte fait* (1972) and *La cérémonie des adieux* (1981) constitute a discursively heterogeneous collection of texts held together by the 'author function' and two chronologies. First, they map onto chronic time in the sense that they recount a life from 1908 up to 1974. Second, they were produced over approximately eighteen years, starting in 1956. The precise chronology of that production is not easy to chart. The texts are sequential in that each volume enters into a relation with the preceding one, modifying, revising or re-emphasising. They are tentacular in that they may refer non-reciprocally to Beauvoir's other writings as well as to events of personal, political and cultural life. A further complication derives from the fact that the texts themselves are an assemblage of disparate texts. The main narrative is fragmented at various points in order to incorporate (often with difficulty in terms of editing or commentary) sections from diaries, notes and letters which are generally contemporary with the point of chronic time reached in the main narrative. Thus, the memoirs present a complexity of production and composition. What is interesting is to take note of that diversity and the drive towards coherence, the textual effort to gain control over its disparateness.

In Beauvoir's case, the question of the narrative organisation of the memoirs is imbricated with philosophical issues. I shall therefore preface my examination of this aspect of the texts with a brief consideration of the importance of literature for Beauvoir and its role within *her* existential project.

We read in *Mémoires d'une jeune fille rangée* that Beauvoir, at the age of fifteen, lost her faith in God and that as a consequence she came into confrontation with the 'nothingness' that is central to existentialism. Surprisingly, the vocabulary of religion does not disappear. Instead, it is displaced onto literature and writing. 'At difficult times in my life, scribbling sentences, even if nobody is going to read them, brings me the same solace as *prayer to the believer*' (TCF, p. 135: pp. 168–9, emphasis added). The *Mémoires d'une jeune fille rangée* are described as the story of 'my literary *vocation*' (FA, p. 8: I, p. 10). This displacement from a God-centred faith to a Man-centred philosophy (existentialism) brought with it the bag and baggage of religion – the hope of immortality and certain moral imperatives: 'For me, the idea of salvation had survived God's disappearance and my first conviction was that each person must personally take care of his own' (FA, p. 62: I, p. 73). According to existentialism, it is the responsibility of each individual to confront the facticity of the world by engaging his or her freedom in a project, in action. For Beauvoir, literature was the domain of that project. In her case, to write was to act and to act was to be. The literary act derives its value from being an existential act. (Consider then the ontological crisis that would follow the news of the death of the author!)

Given the supreme ontological value attached to literature, it is not surprising that the choice of narrative form should also be implicated in the existential project. A footnote in *La force des choses* states that the text is written 'sur un mode historique', that it is 'une chronique' (FC, p. 275: I, p. 360). A few pages later, the question is posed as to why the narrative form is chronological: 'why did I subject myself to the chronological order of events? I thought about it, I hesitated. But what matters most in my life is that time flows on' (FC, p. 288: I, p. 377).

The chronological structure of the autobiographies is discussed in 'Mon expérience d'écrivain'. It is argued that a linear, sequential narrative is appropriate because the existential project is an historical movement of *dépassement* towards the future. The process is perpetual. In life, there is no closure except at the moment of death. The disadvantage of the linear narrative, it is suggested, is that events are strung out along the lines of the text. The reader never gets to 'l'essentiel', is never able to construct meaning. Of course, in 'real life' one thing does lead to another, there is a causal link between past and present. But can this be represented in writing? Are we perhaps misled into accepting the notion of linear determinism in writing by the spatial sequence of lines of words moving from left to right across the page, giving a real sense of a beginning, a middle and an end?

Beauvoir continually engaged with and was troubled by the vexatious question of the relation between reality and its representation. She tried unsuccessfully to theorise a generic difference between novel and autobiography on the basis of an opposition between *nécessité* (which gives the 'why' of how things happened as they did) and *contingence* (which provides the 'how') (FC, p. 511–12: II, pp. 296–7). It would fall to autobiography to represent *la contingence* by deliberately including a mass of trivial detail: 'I thought that instead of eliminating contingent details, facticity, as one does in the novel, you could take the opposite course and make something positive of *contingence*, of *facticité*' (E, p. 449). Of course, the inclusion of trivial details is an artistic device in the service of the representation of *contingence*. Also, Beauvoir realised the consequences of such a course for an autobiography, which would become so cumbersome as to put the reader off. This brought her back to the need to select, with the result that her distinction between novel and autobiography collapsed: 'I am forced to choose. That choice [in autobiography] will be guided by the same principle as in a novel – to bring out a meaning – to retain, therefore the elements, the episodes which will help to highlight it' (E, p. 454).

Elsewhere, Beauvoir writes that what she really wanted to represent was the *process* of the engagement of the *pour-soi* with the *en-soi*. She believed Sartre had achieved this in his autobiography, *Les Mots*, 'I grasped, live, the transition ('le passage') of a contingent story to the timeless necessity of a text' (TCF, p. 55: p. 66).

Despite the perception that writing always organises (selects) and, therefore, that it implicitly does this retrospectively (*nachträglich*) Beauvoir continued to write in a quasi-historical mode (quasi because Beauvoir's historical mode does not conform to Benveniste's criteria, that is, no first- and second-person pronouns and no tenses of discourse).

The only occasion when Beauvoir departs from a linear main narrative is in *Tout compte fait*. Unlike the earlier volumes of autobiography in which both writer and reader are caught up in the desire to narrate and discover what happened next, in the prologue of *Tout compte fait*, Beauvoir proposes to call a halt to this process, to make a closure. This is justified, in my view problematically, by associating the end of the narrative with the end of Beauvoir's life:

> The closer I get to the end of my life, the more possible it becomes for me to embrace as a whole this strange object that is a life. I shall attempt to do it at the beginning of this book. . . . In the preceding volumes I adopted a chronological order. I know the disadvantages of that . . . it seems as if the main point is always ahead, further on. . . . By containing

it in sentences, my narrative turns my life into a finished
reality, which it is not.

(TCF, p. 7: p. 9)

If the trajectory of the narrative of Beauvoir's life is
thought of in terms of the movement of a pendulum,
then the three volumes that precede *Tout compte fait*
represent a single wide swing, one leisurely repetition.
Tout compte fait, in contrast, presents us with a series of
repetitions, as if the pendulum were in the final stages
of its movement, in a state of reduced oscillation. The
narrative is caught between stasis and movement, a
state which allows Beauvoir to write that little has
happened over the years 1962–72 (stasis) and then to
produce over 600 pages largely concerned with them
(movement). The text includes a repetition of the narrative of childhood and youth, but organised more or less
thematically around such topics as the importance of
change in Beauvoir's life, dreams, literature, friends,
travel, cultural and political life.

Beauvoir's autobiographies present a fascinating inter-
action between two narrative modes: a linear, chronological (and chronic) narrative which figures the 'I' of the
énoncé, of the statement, and a discourse which figures the
'I' of the *énonciation*, which retrospectively shapes and
organises the linear narrative (what I call the main
narrative) and whose effect is to undercut its authority. I
shall call this second mode the meta-narrative. I am not
suggesting that these meta-narrative passages are clearly
outside the main narrative. Rather, the relation between
the two is a complex and dynamic one.

I suggested earlier that there might be a discourse in the
autobiographies whose relationship to the main (linear,
apparently deterministic) narrative might be problematic.
The question is whether the meta-narrative might be

considered feminine in the sense that it is marginal to the steam-rollering main narrative (itself constructed as masculine, being chronological, historical, teleological and linear).

I shall try to show how the feminine meta-discourse intrudes upon and disrupts the smooth progression of the main narrative (for a similar effect see Chapter 3, Anne's narrative acting on Henri's), and hence can be thought of as a site of resistance to the masculine. However, the text displays the bind of this conception of the feminine: that is, the feminine, being within the Symbolic order, language, representation, has a complicitous relationship with it. My argument is that in this case the meta-narrative displays the *potential* (and therefore the risk) of replicating the hegemony of the main narrative in that it adumbrates its own (linear) narrative (of the writing process) which could be developed and given explicit chronic and subjective reference.

Against this scenario of the meta-narrative as feminine, it must be pointed out that the meta-narrative is metaphorical and masculine in that it seeks to impose its meanings on the main narrative. And, as I hope to show, such imposed meanings may produce a backlash from the main narrative as the latter fails to 'shape up' to the demands of the meta-narrative.

The meta-narrative passages appear in two locations. They are either set apart from the main narrative and are clearly marked: 'Prologue' in *La force de l'âge* (FA, pp. 7–9: I, pp. 9–11), a preface in *La force des choses* (FC, pp. 5–7: I, pp. 7–10), 'Intermède' in *La forces des choses* (FC, pp. 284–8: I, pp. 373–8), 'Epilogue' in *La force des choses* (FC, pp. 659–74: II, pp. 489–508), 'Prologue' in *Tout compte fait* (TCF, pp. 7–8: pp. 9–10) and 'Preface' in *La cérémonie des adieux*, or they appear within the main narrative in transitory or sustained form, notably in *La force de l'âge* (FA, pp. 359–68: II, pp. 410–22).

What is the function of the meta-narrative? It frames the narrative and discourses on its project. It has the possibility of direct address to the reader and thus to orient the reader in a particular direction. It functions as a supplement to the main narrative in that it can speak of what is repressed there, the work of its production, the writing process.

Honesty and sincerity are much paraded in the meta-narrative – 'If an individual, be he Samuel Pepys or Jean-Jacques Rousseau, humdrum or exceptional reveals himself with *sincerity*...' (FA, p. 8: I, p. 10, emphasis added). Or, 'In general people have recognised a quality in me I was much attached to – a *sincerity* as far removed from boasting as from masochism' (FC, p. 6: I, p. 9). Sincerity, within the context of the auto-biographical project, is marked by the imperative of the confessional to 'tell all'. This demand is negotiated at the beginning of *La force de l'âge*:

> I must warn them [readers] that I do not intend to tell them *everything*. I have omitted nothing in the story of my childhood and youth but if I was able to uncover my distant past without embarrassment and too much indiscretion, I do not have the same feeling of detachment in relation to my adult life, I do not have the same freedom. There is no question of gossiping about myself and my friends. I do not like tittle-tattle, I am determined to leave many things in the dark.
>
> (FA, p. 8: I, pp. 9–10)

The meta-narrative displays a passion for factual accuracy – 'In this book I have agreed to some omissions, never to lies' (FA, p. 9: I, p. 11). Such is the textual anxiety about 'telling all' that the reader is inadvertently guided towards areas of omission (notably Sartre's life). The reader is, in effect, encouraged to focus on such (difficult) matters.

But these passages display another 'sincerity'. They tend to self-de(con)struct due to their (over-)insistence on contentious questions. There is a textual drive to push doggedly on until at last the text acts against its own best interests, makes blatant its contradictions.

This is true of the discourse on autobiography. The meta-narrative passages are the site of an initially benign encounter between author and readers with the main narrative being offered up in response to public curiosity concerning such questions as 'Why do you write? How do you spend your days?' (FA, p. 8: I, p. 10). But even in this first prologue we can see the beginnings of a power struggle between Beauvoir and a section of the public which she saw as increasingly malevolent. It is suggested that the aim of the main narrative is, perhaps, to 'clear up certain misunderstandings which always come between authors and their public' (FA, p. 8: I, p. 10). The implication here is that author and reader have shared interests but that lack of information can sometimes obscure them. The effort to assert the authority of the main narrative and, of course, its author becomes more intense when the text inveighs against what are seen as defiguring representations produced elsewhere, in other discourses (magazine articles, for example). The fact that other representations or versions of the Beauvoir story were being introduced was the result of Beauvoir having become a public figure and public property.

In the Preface of *La force des choses I*, a bid is made for re-(self-)possession which entails the redrawing of the public/private dichotomy by subsuming the former into the latter. The private domain is staked out as a territory which is out of bounds to public gaze and to which only Beauvoir can grant access: 'People also said "We know your story because since '44, it's been public." But this publicity has been only one dimension of my private life and since one of my plans is to clear up misunderstandings, it seems useful to me to give a truthful account of it' (FC, p. 5: I, pp. 7–8).

By the Epilogue at the end of *La force des choses II*, there is evidence of a mounting desperation, paranoia even, at the activity of mythomaniacs who defigure and misrepresent. Ostensibly, the grievances have to do with factual inaccuracies such as the story that Beauvoir and Sartre had secretly married. However, beneath the repeated assertions of the need to set the record straight, to 're-establish the truth', there is a certain disingenuousness, as if *the* truth, Beauvoir's truth, were absolute.

However, a close look at the preface of *La force des choses* shows the text over-reaching and revealing itself. Just as Pepys and Rousseau had been invoked in the Prologue of *La force de l'âge*, so Rousseau pops up here in the company of Rabelais, Saint-Simon and Montaigne. While rejecting the classification of the works of these writers as 'works of art', the text does not challenge the value or position of these writers in the canon of French literature and, indeed, by implication, it seeks to place Beauvoir's memoirs in that pantheon on account of the faithful representation of 'the life'. The following sentence strikingly mimics both the style of Montaigne and his claim to artlessness, 'Non; pas une oeuvre d'art, mais ma vie dans ses élans, ses détresses, ses soubresauts, ma vie qui essaie de se dire et non de servir de prétexte à des élégances' (FC, p. 6: I, p. 8). And there the text would have done well to leave Beauvoir in the company of these illustrious gents – but no, it pushes on, honest to a fault:

> In short, due to the fact that I am not passing judgment on myself, I am not aware of any impediment to throwing

some light on my life – at least in so far as I am positioning myself in my own discourse ('univers'). Maybe if my image were projected into another discourse – that of psychoanalysis, for example – I would be disconcerted or embarrassed. But given that I am the one painting the picture, I am not afraid of anything.

(FC, p. 7: I, pp. 9–10)

Here is a clear indication of the power of the word, of discourse to aestheticise or denigrate. (Could not these words be taken as an invitation to approach the text from the perspective of psychoanalysis?)

The reasons, offered in the meta-narrative passages, for undertaking the autobiographical project are over-determined and ultimately contradictory. They include the recuperation of the past into the materiality of print, an assessment of the meaning of the life lived thus far, a setting the record straight, the presentation of a non-judgemental and faithful account of the life and an open-ended 'wait-and-see' project. If the conscious aim of these passages was to shape and control reader response to the main narrative, I would argue that they produce the opposite effect.

An optimistic reader who may believe that language can unproblematically represent the subject and his or her experience should be disabused when Beauvoir's 'honesty' brings her into confrontation with the splitting of the subject in language, with the non-coincidence of Beauvoir with her representative in language, what she calls elsewhere the '*je* qui parle' and the '*je* vécu' (TCF, p. 130: p. 164): 'As I bring my story to mind, I always find myself above or beyond something which has never been finished' (FC, p. 671: II, p. 504).

The reader reaches a sort of Beauvoirian bottom line in the 'Epilogue' of *La force des choses* when, at a period of deep depression, Beauvoir can find no rational argument or justification for continuing to write – such is the impasse to which life and her spirit of interrogation (not sufficiently recognised) have brought her:

> Despite this fundamental disillusion, with all idea of task, mission, salvation gone, no longer knowing for whom or why I am writing, I need to do it more than ever. I no longer think of it as a justification but without it, I would feel mortally unjustified. . . . Where, at the age of 55, just as it did at 20, does this extraordinary power of the Word come from? I say 'Nothing has happened except what has happened' or 'One and one make one – what a mistake!' and I am exalted as a burning flame rises in my throat.
>
> (FC, p. 666: II, p. 498)

Is this Beauvoir's credo – this evocation of 'le Verbe', the Word, biblical, with Beauvoir as disciple receiving the Holy Spirit at Pentecost, but also the Logos, phallic, erotic, self-sufficient, what Kristeva calls the 'legislating principle' (Kristeva, 1986, p. 143)?

The passage above brings us to Beauvoir's consuming passion – the practice of writing. It is precisely a representation of this process that is lacking in the main narrative and which the meta-narrative seeks to supplement. 'You can scarcely describe work. You do it and that's it. At the same time it takes up so little space in this book whereas it fills so much of my life' (FC, pp. 284–5: I, p. 373). A description follows of the 'labeur pénible' of writing, from rough draft to draft, and so on. If Beauvoir might, with some justification, be accused of myth-making in some areas of her life, it seems to me that here she does an excellent job of demystifying the process of writing.

The meta-narrative passages, on account of their concern with the writing process, actually initiate their own narrative, one which tells of how the main narrative came to be written, the doubts, difficulties and false starts:

> I have said why, after the *Memoirs of a Dutiful Daughter*, I decided to go on with my autobiography. I stopped, breathless, when I had got to the liberation of Paris. I needed to know if my project was of interest. It seemed that it was. Yet, before carrying on with it, again I hesitated.
>
> (FC, p. 5: I, p. 7)

Finally, and again connected with the process of writing, the meta-narrative passages take up the question of narrative form. The dynamic which drives the main narrative is desire, specifically the desire (often attributed to readers as well as to Beauvoir) to learn 'what happened next', and following from that, the desire for an ending, for closure and meaning. The former is repeatedly invoked as a compelling reason for continuing the story: 'Invisible, beneath the last line, there is a question mark that I could not stop thinking about. Freedom – what for? All this fuss and bother, this great struggle, this escape, this victory, what meaning were they to have in my later life?' (FA, p. 7: I, p. 9). But, for Beauvoir, this metonymic chain, with its perpetual deferral of meaning (the main point, 'l'essentiel' is up ahead, further on (TCF, p. 7: p. 9)) is unsatisfactory unless there is an ending, a moment of metaphorical totalisation.

What the meta-narrative does is to rupture the main narrative, disturb its chronology, and open up spaces where the problem of meaning can be addressed and to an extent resolved by the provision of 'stop-gap' or provisional meanings: 'My life is not over, but it already has a meaning that is unlikely to be changed much in the future' (FA, p. 8: I, p. 10), or 'Why is there this pause all of a sudden? I know perfectly well that a life cannot be broken up into separate periods and 1952 was not a cut-off date in mine. . . . My narrative, before I can go on with it, requires a certain bringing into focus' (FC, p. 284: I, p. 373). Of course, such meanings are compromises, temporary, because so long as there is no real closure, death, there is no *last* word. One aspect of this meta-narrative function is the imposition on chronic time of a personal periodisation, as seen in the example above, which makes 1952 a key date in the personal history. Other key dates in the Beauvoir story are 1929, liberation from the 'milieu bourgeois' and 1939, loss of individualism.

What is the effect of the meta-narrative passages on the main narrative? The main narrative is presented in an historical mode. Events are presented sequentially according to their chronological occurrence, implying a linear determinism in which the past produces the present. This is the opposite of a narrative form which seeks, overtly, to present the past from the present, in which an 'I', situated in the present, is privileged as it goes about organising, valorising and constructing the past. This is the 'I' of the *énonciation* and it tends to be confined to the meta-narrative.

However, it casts its shadow over the main narrative in the form of irony which produces a negative certitude. It functions to undercut the 'I' of the *énoncé*, which does appear in the main narrative.

For example, during her teens Beauvoir had been doing voluntary social work and had become disillusioned with it:

> Nevertheless, I concluded that doing something was a spurious solution. By claiming to devote ourselves to others we only seem to get ourselves off the hook. I had no idea that doing something might take a quite different form from what I was condemning. Because even if I had a

feeling that the social work teams were mystificatory, I was, nevertheless, sucked in by them.

(MJFR, p. 225: p. 311)

The first two sentences suggest that Beauvoir had achieved a certain clear-sightedness. But this is undercut by the negative in the third sentence. The judgement made in the final phrase could only be made retrospectively, from some moment posterior to the whole episode.

On occasion, that moment is marked by a deictic, 'Today, what seem to me the most important things about these conversations, was not so much what we said as what we took for granted. These things were not to be taken for granted, we were wrong about almost everything' (FA, p. 14: I, p. 19). 'Today', a deictic, indicates the 'now' of the 'I' of the *énonciation*. We cannot locate it in chronic time. But that does not matter. Its effect is to act on and devalue the 'misguided' certainties of the past. This irony, generated out of the discontinuity or splitting of the two 'I's, functions to cancel meanings produced in the main narrative (of cause and effect). And so, within that narrative, an existential narrative of possibility, meaning is elusive, perpetually displaced.

This difficulty in reading continues throughout the memoirs though in different degrees. In the case of *La cérémonie des adieux*, Beauvoir is consciously Sartre's biographer as well as her own autobiographer. The problematical 'I's are still present but there is an emphasis on an impersonal third person, Sartre. I shall examine this text later in this chapter when I discuss Beauvoir's relationship with Sartre.

I shall be reading the Beauvoir story backwards, taking the beginning of the main narrative as the endpoint of the structuring processes that have produced it. The irony mentioned above may be taken as a teleological gesture enjoining the reader to read on. My plan, then, is to read back into the main narrative the key propositions made in the meta-narrative and to look for the effects – dissymmetries, difficulties of that project. I have chosen to focus on three propositions which will be fully laid out below. Briefly, they are: 1. that by her early twenties, Beauvoir had freed herself from her bourgeois up-bringing; 2. that for Beauvoir, femininity never presented a problem; and 3. that Beauvoir's relationship with Sartre was an unqualified success.

In *La force de l'âge*, we read that *Mémoires d'une jeune fille rangée* had narrated the 'liquidation' of Beauvoir's bourgeois past, 'When I met up with him [Sartre] again in October, I had liquidated my past* – I threw myself unreservedly into our story' (FA. p. 14: I, p. 18). The Prologue of *La force de l'âge* mentions hard-won freedom, escape, struggle and victory. The title, *Mémoirs d'une jeune fille rangée*, suggests, rather less dramatically, that liberation from the 'milieu bourgeois' had been achieved – the 'jeune fille', the conventionally dutiful daughter has been put away, 'rangée'. My reading of the text contests this affirmation of a past, an identity, tidily despatched.

There is no meta-narrative in *Mémoires d'une jeune fille rangée*. Beauvoir considered this text to be 'romanesque', like a novel. The text is curiously lop-sided, for, if it seeks to narrate Beauvoir's struggle for emancipation, it is equally (or more) the story of two similar struggles, both of which ended in total failure, in the premature deaths of the protagonists. Any sense of Beauvoir's success is achieved out of its being presented in counterpoint to the failures of Jacques and Zaza. Beauvoir's

---

'* I had told the story of this liquidation in *Memoirs of a Dutiful Daughter*.'

success is the negative one of not having failed. The function of Jacques' and Zaza's stories within the conscious project of the text explains why such a large proportion of what is offered as an autobiography is taken up with their stories.

Jacques Laiguillon was Beauvoir's cousin. They consequently shared the same background. He is presented as a potential husband for Beauvoir, who, at one stage, thinks that she is in love with him. Jacques' story is introduced in the typically ironic mode described earlier: 'At that time I preferred to feel amazed rather than to understand. I did not try to place Jacques nor to explain him. It is only today that I am putting his story together with a bit of coherence' (MJFR, p. 198: p. 274). It is interesting to see how the process of composition, the aim for some coherence, can be admitted in the case of Jacques, whereas in the case of Beauvoir, it is more difficult to locate outside the meta-narrative passages.

Jacques' family history is interpolated into the text, a necessary preliminary in order to explain the tragic dénouement which comes at the end. Jacques' death is followed by the events leading up to Zaza's death, so that the two tragedies are positioned at the end of the text, twin symbols of the fate which could so easily have been Beauvoir's.

Jacques had become engaged to a rich *bourgeoise*, an arrangement viewed with disgust by Beauvoir and her sister, Hélène: 'For a long time we walked about Paris, sickened to see the hero of our youth being changed into a calculating "bourgeois"' (MJFR, p. 347: p. 484).

The reader might well expect that, with Jacques' complicity with bourgeois ideology, he would disappear from the narrative. This is indeed Beauvoir's first reaction to the news of his engagement: 'In any case that was the end of the story' (MJFR, p. 347:

p. 484). Far from it – the text disrupts its chronology (the chronology of Beauvoir's life mapped onto chronic time), its even progress, in order to follow Jacques to his death many years later. The text recounts the failure of his marriage and business interests, his turning to drink and his penury. A reason other than poor business skills is offered for Jacques' financial difficulties. He had wanted to be innovative and produce in the family glass factory stained glass in the contemporary style of the *arts décoratifs*. His customers, however, continued to demand the 'ugly' old-style products. Rather than bow to market forces and compromise his aesthetic taste, Jacques had allowed the family firm to go into liquidation. He died, prematurely aged and destitute, at the age of forty-six.

Not only does the text digress in order to follow Jacques to his sad end, it also provides a commentary on it, suggesting that his marriage was a self-imposed attempt to conform to the expectations of his class and which ran counter to his 'true nature', and that his business failure was due to his refusal to compromise his aesthetic standards. Jacques is presented as a noble victim, a casualty of his background and who, implicitly unlike Beauvoir, lacked the strength to break free:

> Obviously he got married so as to load himself up with responsibilities. He believed that by sacrificing his pleasures and his freedom, he would make a new man of himself, a man solidly sure of his rights and duties, well-adjusted at home and at work. But voluntarism does not pay. He was just the same, incapable both of shaping up as a bourgeois man and of escaping such an end.
>
> (MJFR, p. 349: p. 487)

Jacques' tragedy is balanced and repeated by Zaza's. It is with the image of Zaza in her coffin that *Mémoires d'une jeune fille rangée* ends. Is Zaza, perhaps, the real 'jeune fille rangée', put away in this definitive and macabre fashion?

Zaza is presented as being more accomplished, original and dynamic than Beauvoir: 'Zaza's gifts were becoming even more pronounced.... My father appreciated, as I did, the style of her letters, the liveliness of her conversation ... I was dazzled by her originality' (MJFR, p. 111: p. 155). Beauvoir is represented as Zaza's negative, 'I loved Zaza so much that she seemed more real than I did – I was her negative' (MJFR, p. 113: p. 158). If 'negative' is read as a photographic metaphor, then Zaza and Beauvoir are produced as aspects of the *same* image, a single representation, in which the positive and negative are interdependent, the one being the condition of the other.

Zaza, like Jacques, had a bourgeois background in common with Beauvoir. Both girls went to school at the cours Désir, which, according to Hélène de Beauvoir, was 'abominable' (Hélène de Beauvoir, 1986, p. 62). At this point in the narrative, the reader might well feel that Zaza will be 'the one who gets away'. She does get away temporarily, to Berlin, from which distance she is able to see her family life objectively. Excerpts from her letters are inserted into the text:

> The utterly respectable conventionality of the lives of most people in 'our milieu' has become intolerable, the more so, since I can remember the time, not so long ago, when I was immersed in it without realising and my fear is that when I go back into that environment, I shall return to that way of thinking.
>
> (MJFR. p. 303: p. 424)

Later, Zaza falls deeply in love with Pradelle. But she feels unable to tell her mother of this love because the latter has, for some time, been trying to persuade Zaza to agree to an arranged marriage. Zaza feels unable to challenge her mother's authority and the interdictions which flow from it. The text implies that Zaza's inability to resolve the dilemma – either to submit to or to contest this maternal authority – results in her illness and death.

The cause of her death is a mystery, 'The doctors talked of meningitis, encephalitis – nobody knew anything for sure. Was it a contagious disease, an accident, or had Zaza succumbed to an excess of tiredness and anxiety?' (MJFR, p. 360: p. 503). The medical causes of death are over-determined and the introduction of the idea of 'anxiety' opens up the possibility of Zaza's death being attributable to the unresolved contradictions imposed on her by her bourgeois background.

Zaza, a second 'jeune fille rangée', faces the same struggle as Beauvoir to assert her autonomy. Her failure is entwined with Beauvoir's success. Beauvoir's sense of achievement is marred by guilt: 'Together we had fought the fateful slough that awaited us and, for a long time, I thought that I had paid for my freedom with her death' (MJFR, p. 360: p. 503).

If Zaza is thought of as Beauvoir's alter ego (remembering the photographic metaphor), then the aggressiveness characteristic of the ambivalent relationship with an alter ego could well manifest itself as guilt, self-reproach. However, I prefer to read the guilt as a consequence of the textual strategy which 'used' Zaza's tragic end as a counterpart and condition of Beauvoir's success.

Zaza's death is tragic because she dies at the wrong time. In fact, she never really lives. Her end almost collapses back into her beginning with the result that the space between (the life) is never fully opened. Zaza's story functions as a sub-plot in the way described by Peter Brooks:

The subplot stands as one means of warding off the danger of short-circuit, assuring that the main plot will continue through to the right end. The desire of the text (the desire of reading) is hence desire for the end, but desire for the end reached only through the at least minimally complicated *détour*, the intentional deviance, in tension, which is the plot of narrative.

(Brooks, 1977, p. 292)

As for the 'real' nature of Beauvoir's relationship with Zaza (Elisabeth Mabille), we can only speculate in the same way, as with Olga Kosakievicz. There is no doubt about the importance of Elisabeth in Beauvoir's adolescent years, nor is there any mistaking the intensity of the affection for Zaza represented in *Mémoires d'une jeune fille rangée*. Hélène de Beauvoir has provided further evidence of the importance of Zaza. She wrote that Simone and she only stayed on at the 'cours Désir' so that Simone would not be separated from Elisabeth.

It is also clear that Beauvoir had an intense desire to tell Elisabeth's story. She made several attempts at it, two of which survive. The first appears in *Quand prime le spirituel* (Anne, Part 4) written between 1935 and 1937 but not published until 1979. The second version appears in *Mémoires d'une jeune fille rangée* and has been discussed above. The two versions are vastly different, and are discussed in Deborah MacKeefe's 'Zaza Mabille: Mission and Motive in Simone de Beauvoir's *Mémoires*'.

Central to the paradox of Simone de Beauvoir with which I began this book is the question of her relation to femininity, specifically to her own femaleness, particularly to her body. The difficulties and contradictions in this relation are probably the most striking effect of the consequences of Beauvoir's masculine position. For her, the question of femininity could not be ignored as it could for Sartre. But it was not addressed in a direct and personal way. On the personal level, it is generally denied as constituting a problem. It does not disappear. It is simply displaced from the personal to the impersonal and becomes the subject of *Le deuxième sexe*. The following quotations are striking for their contradictions and for the repeated use of negatives:

> I did not regret being a girl.
>
> (MJFR, p. 55: pp. 76–7).

> My education had convinced me of the intellectual inferiority of my sex.
>
> (MJFR, p. 295: p. 412)

> Yet I did not deny my femininity.
>
> (MJFR, p. 295: p. 413)

> I did not think of myself as 'a woman' – I was me.
>
> (FA, p. 62: I, p. 73)

> I did not deny my femininity, neither did I assume it – I did not think about it.
>
> (FA, p. 367: II, p. 419)

According to Freud, negation, especially when it is repeated, can be a pointer to what is repressed. In this case, it is the feminine which is repressed with considerable insistence. However, the feminine returns powerfully at various points in the autobiographies, demanding negotiation.

In *Mémoires d'une jeune fille rangée*, Beauvoir and Zaza discuss their futures:

> I had decided long ago to devote myself to intellectual work. I was outraged when Zaza declared provocatively 'Bringing nine children into the world as Mother has done is worth at least as much as writing books.' I could see no basis for comparison between these two destinies. Having children meant always harping on the same old tune – the

educated person, artist, writer, thinker, created another world, dazzling and joyful, where everything had a 'raison d'être'.

(MJFR, pp. 140–1: pp. 195–6)

The text, while insisting on the non-equivalence of artistic creation and procreation actually brings them into confrontation.

The same theme is taken up again in *La force de l'âge* around the issue of whether or not Beauvoir and Sartre should marry. Since neither of them wanted to have children, the argument runs that there can therefore be no reason to marry. End of discussion, the reader might think. But no, the text is insistent, arguing the case for a woman's right to create rather than procreate:

> I have told how outraged I was when we were about fifteen and Zaza asserted that having children was as good as writing books. I continued not to see any common measure between these two destinies. Through literature, I thought, you justify the world by creating it anew in the purity of the imaginary and at the same time you save your own life. Having children is, pointlessly, to increase the number of beings on the earth. Nobody is surprised that a Carmelite, having chosen to pray for all men, should forgo producing individual beings. My vocation did not suffer from any hindrances either and it stopped me following any plan which was unrelated to it.
>
> (FA, p. 78: I, p. 91)

This passage first repeats, almost verbatim, the argument made in *Mémoires d'une jeune fille rangée* – artistic creation and procreation are radically different. The argument is then developed further: unlike procreation, artistic creation is purposeful and salvational. Then a new idea is introduced – the religious vocation. This may seem a gratuitous move until we see its purpose.

For a woman, the religious vocation prescribes chastity and, what is more important, has non-procreation as its corollary. The text sets up the literary vocation as equivalent to the religious vocation, less because they have 'salvation' in common than because the religious vocation has non-procreation as one of its *socially sanctioned* conditions. The text seeks to arrogate this condition to the female writer and in the process becomes symptomatic of the necessity of negotiating the traditional construction of femininity.

The idea of the literary product as equivalent of, or compensation for, producing a child returns in *La force de l'âge*. Beauvoir was thirty when she began to write *L'invitée*, her first published novel: 'In the family and among my childhood friends, there were whispers that I was a barren fruit. My father got cross "If she's got something in her stomach, let her produce it." I was in no hurry' (FA, p. 365: II, p. 416). Beauvoir, I sense, felt that it was imperative to produce a literary work as a compensation for her refusal to conform to traditional femininity, even if, superficially, it seems she has no sense of urgency.

Associated with the issue of reproduction is the question of marriage – a further site of contradiction and difficulty. Musing on what her ideal partner would be like, Beauvoir required that he should be her equal and her superior:

> I wanted everything to be shared between husband and wife. Each was to fulfil for the other the role of exact witness that I had formerly given to God. That excluded the possibility of loving someone different – I would only marry if I met someone who was more accomplished than I, my equal, my double.
>
> (MJFR, p. 145: p. 202)

There is a paradox here which is explained in terms of the assertion that since women belong to an inferior caste, a relation based on equality must take account of this initial inequality:

> Being a member of a privileged species and having the benefit of a head start, I reckoned that if, in the absolute, a man was not worth more than me, then in relative terms, he was worth less. In order to recognise him as my equal he had to be better than me.
>
> (MJFR, p. 145: p. 202)

The argument above is remarkable for the way it takes women's (socially constructed) inferiority as a given. It is surprising also that there is no trace of the irony so prevalent elsewhere in the text. We must remember that *Mémoires d'une jeune fille rangée* post-dates, and therefore should be marked by, *Le deuxième sexe*.

Considerable work needs to be done on the repression of the body and the 'maternal' in Beauvoir's writing. This would further reveal the cost of her identification with the masculine. The body, it seems, is always troublesome, irremediably split from the mind. When Beauvoir played at babies with her dolls, she did so only on condition that 'les aspects nourriciers' (feeding/nurturing the body) were omitted. 'Bodily functions' are set aside early in Beauvoir's life, 'I don't know why, but the fact is that bodily functions [phénomènes organiques'] soon ceased to interest me' (MJFR, p. 56: pp. 77–8). Beauvoir's first menstruation was a traumatic experience principally because of her fear of how her father would react. The internalisation of masculine attitudes to the female body can be seen in Beauvoir's reaction. This insistence of the body is seen as a fall from grace: 'I was horrified that he might

Simone de Beauvoir

suddenly think of me as an organism. I felt I had fallen, permanently' (MJFR, p. 101: p. 141). Much later, her sexually desiring body makes its demands felt:

> I would not have known how to explain why, but the idea of a distance between the emotions of my body and what I had decided frightened me. And just this separation happened. My body had its own moods and I was unable to contain them – their violence overwhelmed my defences.
>
> (FA, p. 63: I, p. 74)

Beauvoir was renowned for the long (and punishing) walks she went on, particularly during her period in Marseilles. One reason for these mammoth rambles may have been an effort to exhaust the body, to bring it into a state of compliance with the mind. Sartre remarked on Beauvoir's complicity with physical tiredness: 'when we go walking, Castor [Beauvoir] goes along with her fatigue, she soaks it up so that it becomes a pleasant, wished-for state' (Sartre, 1983, p. 320).

What is affirmed out of the repression of the body is the intellect, the cerebral (masculine 'qualities'). Could this emphasis on the intellect have something to do with Beauvoir's predilection for the turban? In a letter to Beauvoir, written in October 1939, Sartre quotes from a letter he had received from Tania (Olga's sister), "Thereupon, Castor arrived, handsome as a young Hindou in a turban." . . . I would really like to see this turban' (Sartre, *Lettres*, Vol. I, p. 376). The variety, ubiquitousness (spatial and temporal) of this form of headgear is striking. What is to be made of this head-dress(ing), this covering (veiling?) of this part of the body? Is it, perhaps, to do with displaced modesty? Does it indicate where the 'goods' are? The turban, warrior helmet, is there to protect. Gérard Lefort, in 'La dame au turban', published in *Libération*, thought that the turban enhanced the intellectual physiognomy, being also the sign of a certain discipline, a binding-up. He noted the moment, at Sartre's funeral, when the turban came undone, signifying emotional disorder. A final point on the subject of funerals. In Deidre Bair's account of Beauvoir's funeral we read: 'On Saturday, a small group of people were permitted to file by her bier in the amphitheatre of the Cochin Hospital, where she lay in a *scarlet turban* and matching bathrobe' (Blair, 1986, p. 213, emphasis added).

There are moments in the autobiographies when Beauvoir's specificity as a woman is posed, but it is either presented as irrelevant or else elided. This occurs when Beauvoir is casting around for something to write about:

> I wanted to talk about myself . . . I decided that the first question to arise was – what had being a woman meant for me? At first, I thought I could quickly dispose of it. I had never felt inferior, nobody had ever said to me 'You think like that because you're a woman.' My femininity had never bothered me at all. 'As far as I'm concerned,' I said to Sartre, 'it hasn't counted – so to speak.' 'All the same, you weren't brought up in the same way as a boy. You'll have to take a closer look.' I did and it was a revelation – this world was a masculine world, my childhood had been nourished on man-made myths and I had not reacted in the same way as a boy. I got so interested that I gave up my plan to write a personal confession. I went to do some reading in the *Nationale* and I studied the myths of femininity.
>
> (FC, p. 103: I, p. 136)

Beauvoir would have dismissed the question of gendering as irrelevant to her case had Sartre not insisted on its importance. It is surprising that despite coming to the staggering realisation of the patriarchal organisation of the world, Beauvoir should not have chosen to write about how she had coped with it. Rather, attention is displaced from her particular case to the general condition of women, thus avoiding an interrogation of the effects of gendering on Beauvoir herself. The 'women question' is thus distanced, it becomes the subject of academic research in the *Bibliothèque Nationale*.

Beauvoir almost never writes *as* a woman, instead she writes *about* women. The exclusion of Beauvoir from women as a group permits her to construct *them* as an object of study in which *she* is not personally implicated. Beauvoir is presented as radically *different* from the women she comes into contact with, 'All at once, I met a large number of women over forty ... they lived as "relative beings". Because I was a writer, and because my situation was different from theirs ... I began to realise the difficulties, the false openings, traps, obstacles most women find across their path' (FA, p. 572: II, p. 655). The emphasis here is on the second-hand nature of Beauvoir's knowledge. There is no hint of solidarity, no 'we'. It is not my intention to criticise Beauvoir. That would be inappropriate. We do need to understand Beauvoir's situation both in social and psychosexual terms in the 1940s. Part, at least, of her lack of a sense of contradiction between herself as a woman and the positions available to her at that time was probably due, as she herself says, to her particular situation in the academic, intellectual milieu in Paris, and also to the absence of a feminist discourse at that time. The masculine academic skills which went into *Le deuxième sexe*, producing two tomes of such weightiness that they could not be ignored (by men as well as women), were crucial factors in laying the groundwork for the development of feminism as we know it today.

The autobiographies

All the volumes of autobiography, and especially *Tout compte fait*, construct Beauvoir as a unified subject, continuous over time, place and occupation: 'If I consider the general line of my life, I am struck by its continuity' (TCF, p. 37: p. 44); and 'there are ties which go back a long way and which have never been broken. Basically two things give unity to my life: the place Sartre has always had in it and my fidelity to my original project – to know and to write' (TCF, p. 38: p. 45). Sartre is an important element in that continuity, part of the project, very much the fellow traveller. (It is understandable, therefore, that Beauvoir should have taken it upon herself to complete the narrative of his life.) She wrote in the Epilogue of *La force des choses*, 'There has been one sure success in. my life – my relations with Sartre' (FC, p. 659: II, p. 489). And in *Tout compte fait*, her meeting with Sartre is considered 'the most important event' in her life (TCF, p. 28: p. 33). Since their deaths, the Sartre/Beauvoir couple, the 'premier existential pair' as Angela Carter has called them, have achieved a near-mythological status. How is this relationship presented in the autobiographies? Do they foster the myth-making process? One way of getting some purchase on the question of how they are represented in the autobiographies is to refer, whenever possible, to third parties, other sources.

Sartre makes his appearance towards the end of *Mémoires d'une jeune fille rangée*. He is 'Mr Right', the ideal partner. 'Sartre was just the answer to my prayer as a fifteen year old. He was the double in whom I found all my obsessions brought to a white hot intensity' (MJFR, p. 345: p. 482). Sartre offers Beauvoir a role-model, 'he was, from the word go, the model of what I wanted to become' (MJFR, pp. 145–6: p. 203). The emphasis above is on similarity, the double, and not on difference, which suggests that the relationship will be played out in the Imaginary (see note on pp. 43–4).

Early in *La force de l'âge*, Sartre and Beauvoir conclude their now famous agreement according to which their relation to one another is characterised by Sartre as a 'necessary love' which will always take priority over but will not preclude 'contingent loves'. Part of the agreement was that they would be totally honest with each other (compare with Françoise in *L'invitée*):

> it was thus agreed that we would tell each other everything. . . . I soon realised the advantages of this. I did not need to worry myself any more – a look, definitely benevolent, yet more impartial than my own, returned to me an image of my every movement that I took to be objective.
>
> (FA, p. 24: I, p. 30)

The vocabulary here suggests the 'mirror stage' scenario, the same as that found in the account of the relationship between Françoise and Pierre in *L'invitée*. Sartre and Pierre function in the same way. They return to Beauvoir and Françoise a clear, reassuring image purged of anxiety, that is, from which the Other is absent. But as *La force de l'âge* and *L'invitée* continue, the impossibilities of this situation begin to emerge: 'I had not finally resolved my most serious problem – reconciling my concern for autonomy with the feelings which drove me impetuously towards another' (FA, p. 153: I, p. 177).

Amazingly, Sartre is never seen as 'Other'. But the consequences of this evasion remain to be negotiated, 'the existence of other people remained a danger for me which I did not decide to confront frankly. . . . As for Sartre, I had sorted things out by saying – We are as one. I had placed us together at the centre of the world' (FA, p. 125: I, p. 145). Here, once more, is the romantic

82

cliché which occurred in *L'invitée*. What is missing are the negative aspects of this cosy twosome that Françoise displayed – lack of desire, a sense of dependence.

The romantic cliché appears also in Sartre's letters to Beauvoir. These letters are a valuable source when trying to understand Beauvoir's relationship with Sartre during the early part of the Second World War. They are love letters. They also emphasise Beauvoir's crucial importance as Sartre's literary collaborator. The following extract from one of Sartre's letters, written in September 1939, repeats in more romantic form many of the features of their relationship which I have just noted in Beauvoir's autobiographies:

> Just imagine – when you wrote to me saying that if the worst happened, you wouldn't go on living, it brought me a deep sense of peace. I wouldn't like to leave you behind. . . . It would be as if both halves of a worm that had been cut in two were annihilated. . . . The fact is . . . that I have never felt so strongly that you are me ('vous autre c'est moi'). What is more, when you have lived ten years of your life together and thought the one with the other, the one for the other with never any bad blood between you – it is more than love.
>
> (Sartre, *Lettres*, Vol. 1, p. 290)

Throughout these fascinating letters, Beauvoir (almost always in the masculine) is Sartre's 'petit juge', his 'Castor'.

The Sartre–Beauvoir relationship was obviously quite extraordinary, but this is not to construct it as a 'great love affair'. Olivier Todd called Beauvoir and Sartre the 'frère–soeur siamois' and he noted the similarity in the raucous quality of their voices and the fact that each seemed capable of finishing a sentence begun by the other (Todd, 1981, p. 106).

Within the autobiographies, it is possible to locate and deconstruct this 'unity' in the movement of the shifters, 'I', 'we', and 'he' as they cohere and divide in different configurations.

In *Mémoires d'une jeune fille rangée*, there is a consistent 'I' (however problematical in other ways) until Sartre appears on the scene. By the mid-1940s, when they were both public figures intervening in cultural and political life, there is an alternation between 'I' and 'we'. The problem with 'we' is that it occludes any difference of opinion between the 'I' and the 'you'. This constitutes a particular difficulty for the reader who wishes to disentangle Beauvoir's opinions from those of Sartre. The matter is complicated further when the text claims that to speak of Sartre, 'he', is to speak for both, 'nous': 'For me, problems were posed through him. In this area, I have to speak of him in order to speak of us' (FC, p. 12: I, p. 15).

In a conversation with Sartre and Alice Schwarzer, Beauvoir described her relationship with Sartre as a 'kind of osmosis' (Schwarzer, p. 57). The emphasis was on mutual interdependence and interchange of ideas rather than on a situation in which one person is exerting influence (power and mastery) over the other. It seems unlikely that readers and critics will ever succeed in determining, in some areas, just which of the two was the initiator. Reading both writers, one is struck by their shared commitment to writing, linked, especially in the early days, with a great optimism about the future. They were fellow travellers who knew that they had the same destination.

For Hélène de Beauvoir, they were an exemplary couple. She did, however, warn of the damage they tended to cause to third parties. This does suggest that the 'necessary love' was never seriously threatened.

Albert Memmi disagrees, suspecting that their 'understanding was hard-won and always unstable' (Memmi, 1968, p. 161). Memmi surmises that Sartre's polygamous inclinations made Beauvoir jealous, a jealousy which she suppressed but which re-emerged in a certain vindictiveness in her attitude to Sartre. In answer to Memmi, we can point to evidence from Sartre's letters which shows that his sexual promiscuity did not upset Beauvoir too much since he sometimes recounts his amorous adventures in graphic detail. On one occasion, he informed Beauvoir that he did not make love to Martine Bourdin because 'you told me not to saying "Don't get in a jam"' (Sartre, *Lettres*, Vol. I, p. 192).

There are two moments in the autobiographies when we get a sense of the 'necessary love' being at risk. There is the case of Olga, and there is Sartre's affair with an American woman just after the war. The text never openly confronts the possibility of the primary relationship being ruptured: it exists as a tension just beneath the surface. Textual energy is always channelled into a focus on the third party.

The text holds Beauvoir's two (important) love affairs at a safe distance from Sartre in terms of space and time. The first was with an American, Nelson Algren, and the second with Claude Lanzmann: 'As for me, I needed to be distanced in order to become emotionally involved because there was no question of repeating my understanding with Sartre. Algren belonged to another continent, Lanzmann to another generation' (FC, p. 296: II, p. 16).

La cérémonie des adieux had a mixed reception when it was published in 1981, recounting, as it does, the distressing minutiae of Sartre's physical decline. It is the only volume of autobiography to be written without Sartre, a fact poignantly mentioned in the Preface.

However, while the Preface acknowledges Sartre's absence in 'real life', it also signals his presence in the text which follows. The 'great love story' goes on, in print, beyond the grave! The title, *La cérémonie des adieux*, refers to Sartre's words to Beauvoir on the occasion of their parting to go off on separate summer travels. But beyond that, the whole book is a literary farewell to Sartre, a textual ceremony whose ritual places Sartre alongside Beauvoir for ever. In a moment of literal as well as metaphorical togetherness, Beauvoir recounts how she climbed onto Sartre's bed in order to lie alongside his dead body. This is indeed a moment of high romance cut through by the macabre as we learn that Beauvoir was forbidden physical contact with Sartre because he had had gangrene.

La cérémonie des adieux brings the Beauvoir and Sartre story to a close. The finality of death, Sartre's inexorable decline, serve only to intensify the life, a life which, henceforward, exists in print. Sartre was the real romantic, not Beauvoir. And yet, throughout the auto-biographies, cumulatively, the Sartre–Beauvoir relationship is given the luminosity of a great love affair. In *Tout compte fait*, Beauvoir's meeting with Sartre is seen as inevitable (written in the stars), their love as constant right to the end.

Chapter Three

Les mandarins: the cost of being a history man

I know perfectly well that one lies the whole time in a
novel. But at least one does it in order to be true.

(Jean-Paul Sartre, *Lettres au Castor et à quelques autres*)

Les mandarins was published in October 1954 and later
that year it received one of France's most prestigious
literary prizes, the *Prix Goncourt*. Thus the novel received the imprimatur of the literary establishment.
Without doubt, Simone de Beauvoir had arrived, she
had achieved the status of a 'great writer'.

The interest and value of the text is generally thought
to derive from the representation of the dilemmas and
preoccupations of a group of male intellectuals in Paris
immediately after the Second World War: the historical
context is therefore crucial. A study of the text's reception when it was first published (it appeared in translation in the United States in 1956 and in Britain in 1957)
shows critics interested in the text as more or less
fictionalised historiography. Many readers, especially

outside France, took the novel as a *roman à clef* (an assertion vigorously rejected by Beauvoir) and busied themselves deciding who was who. In fact such literary detectives had a hard time of it since the facts as known do not map readily onto the text. However, the novel does give an impression of 'how we were then'. The dilemma facing Robert Dubreuilh, Henri Perron and friends is how to resolve the contradictions implicit in their perceived necessity, as intellectuals, for political engagement on the one hand, and their requirement to preserve intellectual freedom and integrity on the other. Many review articles focused less on this important interrogative aspect of the text than on what was taken to be the political position it adopted. Some American readers expressed anger at what was taken to be its pro-Soviet stance. Charles Rolo, writing in *The Atlantic* complained: 'how drearily disgusting it is to watch the Mandarins necking with Communist ideas while feverishly chattering about integrity, idealism, *und so weiter'* (Rolo 1956, p. 77).

There was also a tendency to divide the novel into two parts: the public world of post-war politics (a generally male domain) and the novelistic/fictional world of the female protagonists. Critics were then free to praise the representation of the public life and dismiss or marginalise the private, or vice versa. What such critics tended not to do, and what is, in my view, important, is to try to understand how these two aspects of the text interact. This approach is relevant to the question of gender since the division of the text repeats the now well-known dichotomy between public/masculine and private/feminine.

I am taking the historical conjuncture, located (as Dubreuilh puts it in the text) in the 'radical *coupure'* between the periods of the Occupation and post-Liberation, as the pivot of the text since it initiates and is the context for two related dramas. First, it triggers a private drama of subjectivity for Anne Dubreuilh. Her drama is that of the Lacanian subject at that moment (Oedipus again) when it is brought into confrontation with death, that is, on the point of its entry into the Symbolic order and its emergence as a social subject. This drama constitutes a pre-history. It is necessary to have traversed this process, to have taken up one's position in the social formation, before one can become a participant in the second drama, which is the drama of political formations and realignments in post-war Paris (a history). Both dramas are set, metaphorically, at a crossroads. For Dubreuilh, French intellectuals at that time were 'at the crossroads' (LM, p. 49: p. 59) and for Jacques Lacan, the mirror stage with its associated feelings of love and aggressivity constitute also a 'sort of structural crossroads' (Lacan, 1977, p. 19).

Before proceeding to my reading of the text, I shall examine what Beauvoir wrote about the structure of the novel, especially its bipartite form. In *La force des choses*, she wrote that literature's role is to 'reveal ambiguous, separate and contradictory truths' and that 'only a novel was capable . . . of drawing out the swirling multiplicity of meanings in that changed world I woke up in in August 1944' (FC p. 275: I, p. 360). According to Beauvoir, the text was 'neither an autobiography nor a reportage but an "evocation"' which 'did not give an answer' to the problems her protagonists faced (FC, p. 282: I, p. 369). It was intended to be an interrogative text.

The plot was seen in terms of a rupture and then a reconciliation between two men, Robert Dubreuilh and Henri Perron. Anne's position in relation to Robert, her husband, and Henri's political project is stated paradoxically: she is simultaneously 'deeply engaged in the struggles' and yet is 'exterior' to them (FC, p. 276: I, p. 362). Beauvoir stated that she made Anne the repository of her negativity, her sense of death and taste for the absolute while Henri represents the positive: 'I gave Henri my *joie de vivre*, enthusiasm for getting involved, pleasure in writing. He is at least as like me as Anne, perhaps more so' (FC, p. 280: I, p. 367). Henri did well out of this division of character traits. Not only is he a writer, he is a highly successful one, as is Dubreuilh.

Interestingly, Beauvoir felt the need to justify this privilege: 'In describing a writer, I wanted the reader to see in him a fellow man ['un semblable'] and not a weird animal – a woman whose vocation is writing is much more of an exception than a man' (FC, p. 276: I, p. 362). As we saw in Beauvoir's discussion with Zaza concerning maternity and the profession of writing, reproduction and literary creation are thought inimical to one another (see pages 74–5). However, Beauvoir also wrote that Anne Dubreuilh had an important role because 'a large number of the things I wanted to say had to do with my being a woman' (FC, p. 276: I, p. 362). Note the personal pronoun 'my' above – surprising, since what is specific to Beauvoir is surely her literary vocation. The thorny problem of being a woman *and* a writer is evaded by this strategy of splitting.

Two narratives, Henri's and Anne's, alternate. Beauvoir's intention was not that they should simply alternate but that there should exist what she called a 'counterpoint' between them (FC, I, p. 363). Beauvoir used the same musical metaphor in 'Mon expérience d'écrivain': 'if I am writing a novel, I can perfectly well sustain . . . two themes at once, just like several themes can be sustained simultaneously in a symphony, in a sonata – in counterpoint' (E, p. 444). This is the principle which Bakhtin noted in Dostoevsky's work, 'point versus point (punctum versus punctum) ... *different voices singing in different ways on the same theme'* (Bakhtin, 1973, p. 36). *Les mandarins* is a dual-voiced novel with a double articulation of the same theme (unlike Beauvoir's autobiographies which are mono-vocal). The focus of my reading of the text will be the way in which this counterpoint functions, articulated as it is with the issue of gender.

I have already noted Henri's first privilege – he is a successful writer. His second privilege has to do with narrative style. Quite simply, he goes first. His narrative introduces and situates the protagonists and sets the 'story time' in motion. His narrative is written in the apparently authoritative third person, often with verbs in the past-historic tense (the tense of narrative without a narrator).

This contrasts with Anne's narrative which begins half-way through the first chapter, and which uses predominantly the tenses of discourse (especially the perfect tense). This renders her narrative subjective and less authoritative than Henri's. However, Henri's narrative, despite seeming to be impersonal because of the use of the third-person form, in fact does represent his consciousness and his point of view through the use of indirect free speech.

On page 33: 38 of Chapter 1, there is a switch from Henri's narrative to Anne's. The reader must initially be confused when confronted with a dramatic change of mood and style. First, there is an enigmatic first person, 'No, I shan't meet death today. Not to-day or any other day. I'll be dead for others and yet I'll never have known death' (LM, p. 33: I, p. 38). The reader of the text in French will know that the speaker is a woman because of the feminine ending on 'dead' (second sentence above). Anne can only be identified (named) by reference to Henri's narrative – Henri scores again, his narrative as source of knowledge. The temporal reference of Anne's narrative is also difficult to locate. Her utterance occurs 'today' but how does this relate to the precise chronic reference of Henri's narrative ('the first Christmas after the end of the war')? I think that there are two chronologies here, similar to those found in the autobiographies: masculine/chronic time (Henri's narrative and the main narrative in the autobiographies) and feminine/linguistic time (Anne's narrative and the meta-narrative passages in the autobiographies).

Even Anne's spatial location is a mystery until, some seven pages into the narrative, she says, 'I press my cheek against the pillow' (LM, p. 38: I, p. 45). With the help of such clues, the reader concludes that it is Anne, Dubreuilh's wife, whose voice is represented. She is back home after Paule and Henri's party.

Alone in her room, she is unable to sleep. The momentum of Henri's linear narrative is here suspended. In this half of the first chapter, nothing happens in the way that it does in the first half. Anne never initiates her own chronic story time (as she does subsequently) by breaking through her isolation and going to speak to her husband who is at work in the adjoining room. Anne is immobile (in bed throughout), alone with her thoughts. Chronic time is ticking away next door, but it is never instituted. A careful reading of Anne's narrative makes it almost impossible to establish even a chronology of linguistic time. The point is that Anne is unconstrained by time. Her thoughts run free. They range over time long past, the recent past and the future. She observes no chronology. Her thoughts are organised according to a different principle.

This first chapter is atypical. Anne is never again so radically and sustainedly alone, except at the end of the novel when she contemplates suicide. Throughout the novel, the two narratives alternate, chapter by chapter, with the result that the reader is often given two versions of the same event. This makes for a syncopated rhythm and means that the reader must work to synchronise the two versions welding them together into a single narrative. In Chapter 7, for example, there is an account of a rehearsal of Henri's play (Henri's narrative) followed by Anne's version of the same event in Chapter 8.

Anne is further disadvantaged in this opening chapter. She tends to devalorise her own discourse. This has principally to do with her attitude towards psychoanalysis, her profession.

It is fascinating that Beauvoir makes Anne a psychiatrist. Both Beauvoir and Sartre had a passionate interest in the human mind and behaviour. They could not, however, take psychoanalysis seriously because the concept of the unconscious was antithetical to existentialism. Beauvoir, aware of the problem wrote:

> One of our contradictions was that we denied the unconscious ... and despite our resistances, Freud himself, had convinced us that in every human being there is a core of darkness – something which does not succeed in breaking through social routine or the common-place of language but which sometimes bursts out, scandalously.
>
> (FA, p. 129: I, pp. 149–50)

Beauvoir spoke of her interest in psychoanalysis in an interview with Alice Schwarzer: 'there's something else I would very much like to do if I were thirty or forty now, and that is a work on psychoanalysis' (Schwarzer, 1978, p. 88). Anne's profession is early evidence of this interest. What is more, I think Anne represents a site of contradiction where psychoanalysis (of the adaptive, normative variety) and certain ontological and metaphysical questions could be worked through. Anne sees her professional role as that of helping her patients adapt to the traumas which the war has produced in them, 'I quiet fears, harness dreams, restrain desires: I make them adjust themselves. But to what? I can no longer see anything around me that makes sense' (LM, p. 38: I, p. 45).[1] Not only Anne's patients, but a large number of her friends are traumatised. Sezenac is on drugs, Scriassine has nightmares, Lambert is in a state of conflict at the thought that his father may have denounced Rosa, a Jewish woman whom he loved. Nadine is disturbed, partially on account of the fact that Diego, her Jewish lover, has been deported and killed. The problem is that Anne's therapies tend to dull her patients, depriving them of that stimulus which would make them confront their situation and, in existential terms, assume it. It is the sense of the magnitude of the task and the inadequacy of psychoanalysis to perform it, that forces Anne to turn in on herself and pose fundamental metaphysical questions. It must be emphasised that Anne's process of anguished introspection does not occur in an historical void. Quite the reverse.

She begins by producing her own brief psychobiography, which concludes: 'Nothing in all this is entirely inexact. There I am then, clearly catalogued and willing to be so, adjusted to my husband, to my profession, to life, to death, to the world and all its horrors; me, precisely me, that is to say, no one' (LM, p. 39: I, p. 46). Anne's attitude to psychoanalysis is ambivalent, to say the least. But we must remember that this undercutting of a certain practice of psychoanalysis is done in the course of a lengthy interior monologue, that is, *in private*. In public, when she is talking to Scriassine at the party, Anne asserts the (apparent) mastery of the analyst. '"Don't try analysing me; I know every dark recess of myself. I'm a psychiatrist"' (LM, p. 48: I, p. 58).

Anne's doubts about her profession are just one aspect of a textual process which devalorises her discourse. The process continues with Dubreuilh's emphasis on the fact that Anne has had a lot to drink at the party. Initially, this state of inebriation provides Anne (and the reader) with a reason for marginalising her discourse, 'I'm tired, I drank too much; just a little four-o'clock-in-the-morning frenzy. But who's to decide at what hour one sees things clearest?' (LM, p. 34: I, p. 39). This question prepares the reader for an interesting reversal: 'The walls were spinning, but I was thinking very lucidly, much more lucidly than I do in the morning before breakfast. In the morning before eating, you're on the defensive, you manage somehow to know things you really do know. Suddenly I saw everything with perfect clarity.' (LM, pp. 54–5: I, p. 65.)[2]

Thus the reader, having traversed a gamut of textual strategies which would marginalise Anne's narrative (its subjective first-person narrative; Anne as victim of the 'silly goose syndrome' when, for example, Dubreuilh gently chides her for being worried by Scriassine's analysis of their situation and prefaces his remark by saying, 'A great big girl like you . . .' (LM, p. 51: I, p. 60); Anne as self-deprecatory about her profession and clarity of mind) comes finally to a valorisation of her discourse, however tentative and hedged with doubt.

With the suspension of Henri's story time (a disruption), Anne's narrative opens up the space for a private, subjective and reflective discourse (intra-subjective)

which subtends the public domain (intersubjective)
where Dubreuilh and Perron act.

The purpose of the party attended by Anne and
friends was to celebrate the end of the war. Rather than
the cause of happiness, for Anne it provokes acute
anxiety. She is haunted by thoughts of death. Her
discourse is structured around the notion of death and
associated with it are the problems of identity, truth,
meaning and the future. Like Françoise in *L'invitée*,
Anne asks 'Who am I?' Her first response is to assert her
lack of identity which she then tries to use as a carapace,
'To be no one ... is something of a privilege' and 'I
congratulated myself for not being someone' (LM, p. 39:
I, p. 46). By this retreat into negativity, Anne hopes to
escape the necessity of engaging herself with others
(intersubjectivity). Her meeting with Scriassine at the
party forces her to confront this problem:

> I pressed my lips together, hoping it would prevent me
> from asking further questions. I've always been able to
> avoid being caught by the snare of mirrors. But the glances,
> the looks, the stares of other people, who can resist that
> dizzying pit? I dress in black, speak little, write not at all;
> together, all these things form a certain picture which
> others see. I'm no one. It's easy of course to say 'I am I.' But
> who am I? Where find myself?
>
> (LM, p. 48: I, p. 57)

So Anne plans to keep her mouth shut: by refusing to
speak, she is resisting becoming (a) subject (in)to language. Notice that this refusal extends to writing. The
passage above articulates Anne as split subject in the
disjunction between the first-person pronouns. Anne's
case is indeed grave. By saying that she is 'nobody', we
note that she lacks even that 'subjective certainty'
possessed by the individual prior to the Hegelian

master/slave struggle and which, after the fight, may be transformed into truth:

> Each of these two human-individuals is, to be sure, subjectively certain of himsef; but he is not certain of the other. And that is why his own subjective-certainty of himself does not yet possess truth, i.e. it does not yet reveal a reality – or, in other words, an entity that is objectively, *intersubjectively*, i.e. universally, recognized, and hence existing and valid.
>
> (Kojève, 1980, pp. 10–11, emphasis added)

In order to become a truly 'human person' in the Hegelian sense, Anne must engage in that struggle which seeks to make the 'other' recognise one's desire. Anne, though she recognises the 'call to arms', the look, shrinks from the challenge – an existential no-hoper!

Scriassine's challenge to Anne is two-fold. On an individual intersubjective level, he occupies the place of the Other and is thus able to provoke a personal crisis. He also presents a threat on the collective level. The threat is structurally similar in both cases. Scriassine is a Russian who has spent the war years in the United States. Suddenly, with the Liberation, the isolation (the closed world of Imaginary relations) in which French intellectuals had lived during the war was at an end: 'We had all been living together in such a tightly sealed circle for so long a time, with no intrusions by outsiders, any witnesses, that this man from without troubled me' (LM, p. 43: I, p. 51). Scriassine's look comes from 'another place', outside France. He functions to throw the identity of Dubreuilh and friends into question. The issue for the latter is whether or not writing is a valid activity given the historical moment:

> If men like Dubreuilh and Perron look the situation
> square in the face, they'll become involved in things that
> will demand all their time, all their energies. Or if they
> cheat and obstinately continue to write, their works will be
> cut off from reality, and deprived of any future.
>
> (LM, p. 47: I, p. 56)

It would be wrong to take the sort of introspection Anne is engaged upon as an exclusively female phenomenon in the novel. Henri too is trying to find out who he is. He contemplates writing of ' "what I liked, what I like, what I am," ' . . . Who was he? What manner of man would he discover after that long absence?' (LM, p. 67: I, p. 82).[3] Somewhat later he studies a feature about himself in a weekly magazine. His hope is that the article will function as a message from the Other and tell him who he is: 'reading those printed words, he felt a little of the naive faith of a peasant reading the Bible. It was as if he had succeeded at last in discovering himself through the words he himself had fathered' (LM, p. 156: I, p. 191).[4] Predictably, Henri finds his own message returned to him, deformed. He considers that he has been misrepresented, turned into 'an inferior Rastignac' (a character in Balzac's *Comédie Humaine*).

Paule too is in search of herself and believes that after electroconvulsive therapy she has 'got herself together'. As she remarks to Anne, ' "It wasn't easy, what I went through, but if only you knew how happy I am to have finally found myself!" ' (LM, p. 652: II, p. 352). Unfortunately, her optimism is misplaced. The text makes clear that as a result of undergoing a barrage of therapies, Paule has become 'that fat woman with the sweaty face and the bovine eyes . . . swilling scotch' (LM, p. 653: II, p. 353).

But of all the protagonists, Anne is the most acutely anxious (to the brink of suicide) about her sense of identity and about wider issues such as the way in which the notions of 'truth' and 'meaning', previously fixed and certain, suddenly seem threatened. For Anne, at this time, the world is disorganised, chaotic. She repeatedly notes how certain stars have begun dancing around the heavens or how milestones have shifted. Dubreuilh had always represented a fixed point for Anne, but, by the end of Chapter 1, she begins to doubt even him. 'No fixed stars, no milestones. Robert is a man, a fallible, vulnerable man of sixty whom the past no longer protects and the future menaces' (LM, p. 57: I, p. 68).

Anne's dogged quest for lost truth and meaning is the most manifest evidence in the novel of a feminine discourse, whose effect can be to problematise the assumptions which are taken for granted on the public stage. Dubreuilh stands as a sort of benchmark for the other protagonists. He does not seem to suffer from doubt. For him, the truth can be proved by the presence of incontrovertible evidence. He demands such evidence before he will believe in the existence of the Soviet labour camps. For Dubreuilh, truth is neither relative nor duplicitous. His problem is of a different order. Having located the truth, the question is the ethical one of deciding whether to tell it or not, ' "either you speak the truth or you don't. If you can't make up your mind to speak it always, the best thing to do is to remain silent"' (LM, p. 541: II, p. 200).

Right across the text, the reader encounters the truth as inaccessible or slippery. Take, for example, the point at which Henri lies for a collaborator in order to protect Josette, his new lover. First, the magistrate's office is constructed as a stage which 'seemed to him less real than a theatrical set. The magistrate, the clerk were merely actors in an abstract drama; they were playing their parts. Henri would play his. The truthful word meant nothing here' (LM, p. 628: II, pp. 320–1). As a result of Henri's perjury, what was the truth *for* Yvonne and Lisa (whose evidence Henri had utterly contradicted) disintegrates. The text shows their confusion and perplexity as they alter their original statements in order to bring them into conformity with Henri's evidence.

Lewis Brogan, Anne's American lover, says, after she has discovered he has lied to her, ' "Whether you lie or whether you don't, the truth is never said" '. And later, ' "the worst lie of all [is] pretending that people tell each other the truth" ' (LM, p. 586: II, pp. 262–3). Or consider Henri's thoughts about Josette, 'Even when she lied, she was more truthful than Paula, who never lied' (LM, p. 390: I, p. 487).

Truth, as a sliding signifier, comes to a halt for Anne at the end of the text:

> No! I've denied enough, forgotten enough, fled enough, lied enough. Once, one single time and forever, I want to make truth triumph. Death has won; death is now the only truth. A single move and that truth will become eternal.
>
> (LM, p. 760–1: II, p. 498)

Truth, for Anne, is the recognition of death. The text finally reveals, makes present, that radical absence.

The notion that a message has a fixed meaning intended by the person who produced it also comes under threat, opening up the possibility of plural interpretations. For Henri, therefore, the text of his novel unequivocally represents the truth of his relationship with Paule. But she 'misreads' it, saying simply that it is masterly. What is more, Paule also misreads the simple and direct letter which Henri sends her in which he tells her that their affair is over:

'Can you make anything out of it?' she asked.

'He was afraid to speak to you,' I replied. 'He preferred sending you a letter.'

'But what does it *mean*?'

'It seems clear to me.'

'You're lucky.'

She looked at me questioningly, and finally I muttered, 'It's a letter breaking things off.'

'Breaking things off? Did you ever see a letter that broke things off like this?'

'There's nothing extraordinary about it.'

She shrugged her shoulders. 'Please! And besides, what's there to break between us?'

(LM, pp. 536–7: II, p. 194)[5]

Although the reader is not left in any doubt that Henri does indeed perjure himself and that Paule misreads the letter, still, truth and meaning, as fixed concepts, are seen to shift. It's all a matter of point of view (position).

Returning now to Anne's narrative in Chapter 1, Anne asserts that she is not narcissistic, 'To my Catholic upbringing I owe a highly developed super ego – the reason for my puritanism and my lack of narcissism' (LM, p. 39: I, p. 46). Her mention of the 'snare of mirrors' during her encounter with Scriassine is only one of many references to mirrors throughout the text. Their presence continually returns the reader to the mirror as a metaphor for narcissistic capture and thus to the problems of subjectivity.

Paule's studio is hung with large mirrors. Before their guests arrive, Paule and Henri dance together. Paule reminds Henri of their visit to the 'Palais des Mirages'. Their being together in her studio, reflected in the mirrors, is a repetition of that earlier occasion:

101

She pressed her forehead against his cheek. 'I can see us the way we were then.'

And so could he. They had stood together on a pedestal in the middle of the Palais des Mirages and everywhere around them they had seen themselves endlessly multiplied in a forest of mirrored columns. Tell me I'm the most beautiful of all women.... You're the most beautiful of all women.... And you'll be the most glorious man in the world....

Now he turned his eyes towards one of the large mirrors. Their entwined dancing bodies were infinitely repeated alongside an endless row of Christmas trees, and Paula was smiling at him blissfully. Didn't she realise, he asked himself, that they were no longer the same couple?

LM, p. 13: I, p. 14)

Paule is utterly trapped, seeking the complicity of Henri, her Prince Charming, as a support for her fantasy, her fairytale existence ('Mirror, Mirror, on the wall...'). When, much later in the novel, Paule accepts that everything is finished between her and Henri, she breaks all the mirrors in her studio (LM, p. 553: II, p. 216).

These same mirrors present no threat to Dubreuilh who can joke about them: 'It annoyed her [Paule] when Dubreuilh called her studio a brothel – because of all the mirrors and these red draperies, he said' (LM, p. 14: I, p. 15). Paule is a haunting and horrific representation of the fate of a woman who tries to conform to a traditional construction of femininity when her lover no longer wants her. Paule represents a version of the 'amoureuse' (see Le deuxième sexe, Part Two, III). Anne is on the same slippery slope as Paule (Beauvoir saw Paule as a foil to Anne) who is, at the very bottom, driven to insanity followed by inanity. At the beginning of the novel, however, Paule seems content, though the reader is never left in any doubt that she is deluding herself about Henri and their 'great love'. Anne, in stark contrast, is uneasy, watchful and self-critical.

What evidence is there for suggesting that Anne is narcissistic, that she is one of a line of women in Beauvoir's texts (including Françoise in *L'invitée* and Beauvoir in the autobiographies) to be caught up in the same problematic? Like Beauvoir in the autobiographies, Anne recounts her loss of religious faith at fifteen and the ensuing anguish. This vanished when she met Dubreuilh: 'From the moment I fell in love with Robert, I never again felt fear, of anything. I had only to speak his name and I would feel safe and secure' (LM, p. 33: I, p. 39). Through Dubreuilh, Anne rediscovered the world, *through his eyes* (she does the same thing in the United States with Brogan). In existential terms, Anne lives an inauthentic existence (despite having a profession of her own), because she lives in and through Dubreuilh. What defines Dubreuilh, for Anne, is his identity as a writer. Scriassine's dire warnings about French intellectuals and the relevance of writing throw into relief Anne's narcissistic relation to her husband. It should be noted that although Dubreuilh and Scriassine have different political positions (Scriassine is sympathetic to the United States), both men agree that writing may not be the most appropriate form of intervention at that moment. When faced with this argument, Anne contests it vigorously. She is determined that Dubreuilh should continue to write. Anne is less concerned with writing as a means of political intervention than as a means of transcending death:

> When I was an adolescent, I preferred books to the world of reality, and something of that has remained with me – a taste for eternity. Yes, that's one of the reasons why I take

Robert's writings so much to heart. If they perish, both of us will once more become perishable; the future will be nothing but the grave.

(LM, p. 65: I, p. 77)

For Anne, Dubreuilh's project, his identity, are also hers, 'he is the world for me' (LM, p. 50: I, p. 59). Her identity crisis encompasses him, 'I no longer know who we are' (LM, p. 33: I, p. 39). Anne identifies with Dubreuilh as an alter ego. As a writer, he represents what Anne 'would like to be' (one of Freud's narcissistic types). She guards and defends his projects most zealously because they are her own. What is particularly alarming about Anne's relationship with Dubreuilh is the fact that no distance seems to have opened up between her and him: 'I've never tried to measure him. For me the measure of all things was Robert. I've lived with him as I've lived with myself, *no distance separating us*' (LM, p. 57: I, p. 68, my emphasis).[6] It is as if the spatialising function of the mirror stage has not worked so that self and other are collapsed together.

There is another revealing feature concerning Anne's relationship with Dubreuilh in the first chapter. Anne begins her narrative by recounting a childhood dream (the same fairytale occurs in the autobiographies). The little mermaid, having sold her immortality for the love of a young man, is changed into foam on the seashore. There is a second reference to the mermaid at the end of Chapter 1, but this time Dubreuilh is the mermaid: 'And what then? What will become of him? It's awful to think of a living creature turning into foam' (LM, p. 64: I, p. 76). Dubreuilh reduced to silence, to nothingness, or Anne – it comes to the same thing.

Against all that Dubreuilh himself can say to her, Anne strenuously seeks to preserve Dubreuilh's commitment to writing. To accept that writing had become irrelevant would mean the abandonment of her fiction. Anne's dialogue with Dubreuilh functions at the level of the 'parole vide' because, for her, he does not exist as true Other. We see the strategies she uses to convince herself, against what Dubreuilh says, that all is well: 'He never hides anything from me, but sometimes he keeps certain worries temporarily to himself' (LM p. 49: I, p. 59). Because she does not want to believe what he tells her, she looks for evidence to doubt his words: 'His voice sounded too confident'. And a page further on, she finds his voice 'too reassuring' (LM, pp. 52–3: I, pp. 62–3). Anne even refuses to believe him: 'It's useless for him to protest; above all else he's a writer' (LM, p. 54: I, p. 64). Or else she seeks to convince herself that her thoughts are identical to his, 'Yes, I'm sure he's already told himself everything I've been thinking' (LM, p. 65: I, p. 78).

Paule represents the psychotic endpoint of the sort of relationship that exists between Anne and Dubreuilh. Paule believes she is living a 'great love'. She sees Henri as her creation: 'I created him as he creates characters in his books' (LM, p. 238: I, p. 293). For Paule, their union (back to the romantic cliché 'We are as one') is a mystical affair. ' "You speak as if Henri and I were two distinct beings," she replied dreamily. "Perhaps it's a kind of experience that's simply incommunicable"'. And a few lines further on, ' "fundamentally, we're one single being"' (LM, p. 239–40: I, p. 295). Paule describes this love relation by saying, ' "We're like those earthworms one vainly cuts in two"' (LM, p. 241: I, p. 297). (The same image occurs in one of Sartre's letters Beauvoir, see page 83.) Total self-negation fails to solve Paule's problem, and so she is brought to insanity and the impasse from which she has no satisfactory escape. She has two options: ' "should I take a dose of prussic acid

or try to redeem myself?"' (LM, p. 554: II, p. 217). At
the end of the novel, Anne faces a similar choice. The
suicide connection between the two women is emphasised by the metonymy of transferring the phial of
poison from Paule's handbag to Anne's glove box.

As Elaine Marks wrote in *Simone de Beauvoir: Encounters with Death*, 'the question Anne asks . . . is "how shall
we live?" – the subject of *Les mandarins* – is really the
question of how to live with death' (Marks, 1973, p. 70).
Indeed, it says in the text that death is on the prowl.
Anne's thoughts and reminiscences are structured
around it. No matter which way her thoughts turn, she
encounters its insistent reminders. For most of those
who go to Paule's party, it is an occasion for celebration:
the celebration of the end of the war and of life over
death. As Audet notes in *Simone de Beauvoir face à la
mort*, 'Celebration in Simone de Beauvoir always takes
on a ritual meaning, it becomes a sort of temporary
exorcism of death' (Audet, 1979, p. 59). This is not the
case for Anne. For her, the party is not an affirmation of
life but the manifestation of death, registered in the roll-
call of the dead, those who are absent: Diego, Rachel,
Rosa, Jacques and many others:

> Tonight's a holiday, the first Christmas of peace, the last
> Christmas at Buchenwald, the last Christmas on earth, the
> first Christmas Diego hasn't lived through. We were danc-
> ing, we were kissing each other around the tree sparkling
> with promises, and there were many, oh, so many, who
> weren't there.
>
> (LM, p. 34: I, p. 40)

How does death function in Anne's narrative and in
the text as a whole? Death is seen as absence, quite
literally the opposite of presence: those present at the
party contrasted with the absent dead. Recognition of

death/absence has a crucial function in the process whereby the subject accedes to language, the social domain. Death is the fourth term in the Oedipal process which propels the subject into language, enjoining him/her to speak from the 'I'. Anne's perception of absence takes us to Lacan's rereading of Freud when the latter described his grandson's game with a cotton reel (the *Fort/Da* game), the game in which the child substituted the two syllables in place of the material presence and absence of the mother (a first symbolisation). As Anthony Wilden comments:

> Lacan sees this phonemic opposition as directly related . . . to the binary opposition of presence and absence in the child's world. . . . For the object to be discovered by the child it must be *absent*. At the psychological level the partial object conveys the lack which creates the desire for unity from which the movement toward identification springs – since identification is itself dependent upon the discovery of *difference*, itself a kind of absence.
>
> (Wilden, 1981, p. 163)

Anne seems to be in a state of anguished paralysis in the face of her registering the opposition presence/absence.

This preoccupation with death is perhaps evidence of the powerful existence within Anne of the death instinct. According to Freud in 'Beyond the Pleasure Principle', what the subject desires most of all is to return to the inorganic state where tensions are reduced to nothing. It is a desire for reunion with the lost object (the maternal breast), for a state of non-differentiation, a-subjectivity, annihilation, death. Throughout the novel Anne struggles against/with death. It is only at the very end that she can admit she desires it: 'I press my cheek against the warm grass; I say softly "I want to die." The tenseness in my throat disappears, I suddenly feel very calm' (LM, p. 757: I, p. 493). And:

> But once more . . . death is stalking me . . . I no longer have the strength to flee. To escape a few days of waiting, the condemned man hangs himself in his cell. And I'm supposed to wait patiently for years! What for? I'm tired. Death seems much less terrible when you're tired. If I could die of the longing I have for death, I should take advantage of it.
>
> (LM, p. 757: II, pp. 493–4)

Anne's recognition of death at this late stage makes it possible for her to perceive a distance separating her from Dubreuilh, and further to break out of the Imaginary by stating that that distance is impassable (no endless exchange between self and other):

> For twenty years, I believed we were living together; but no, each of us is alone, imprisoned in his body . . . with his death which ripens noiselessly inside him and which separates him from everyone else.
>
> (LM, p. 758: II, pp. 494–5).

> I walked towards the house, I slipped noiselessly past Robert's window. He is sitting at his desk; he is working. How close he is! How far away! I need only to call him and he'll smile at me. And then what? He would smile from a distance – an impassable distance.
>
> (LM, p. 760: II, p. 497).

In general, the death instinct manifests itself as the compulsion to repeat. For Beauvoir, 'one of the main themes' of the book was 'repetition as Kierkegaard meant the word – to truly possess something, you have to have lost it and found it again' (FC, p. 282: I, p. 369). Beauvoir was referring to Perron and Dubreuilh who, at the end of the novel, return to square one, older and wiser, yet ready to start all over again. Anne finds this compulsion to repeat unacceptable. Like the man in the condemned cell, she would short-circuit the system: 'My fingers tightened around the vial. . . . I will drink. If not, everything will begin again. I don't want it to. Everything will begin again; once more, I'll find my thoughts in order always in the same order' (LM, p. 760: I, p. 497). Anne, as locus of the feminine, articulates here the high cost of living in the phallic order, the domain of 'reason which maintains order: the past behind, the future ahead' (LM, p. 760: I, p. 498): the domain also of time and of history.

Anne's case is an extreme example of the blending of the life instinct and the death instinct, with the latter massively predominating. As Laplanche and Pontalis point out, 'The fusion of instincts [life and death] is a true mixing in which each of the two components may be present in variable proportion' (Laplanche and Pontalis, 1980, p. 180). The death instinct in its pure form represents an innate tendency to self-destruction. However, when fused with the life instincts, the death instinct is turned outwards in the form of aggressiveness: 'The libido has the task of making the destroying instinct innocuous, and it fulfils the task by diverting that instinct to a great extent outwards. . . . The instinct is then called the destructive instinct, the instinct for mastery or the will to power' (Laplanche and Pontalis, p. 98).

Anne does not display the Hegelian will to power. Her reluctance to engage in a struggle with Scriassine shows a low level of aggressivity (a meagre measure of Eros, the life instincts, in her psychic economy?). It comes as no surprise to see the near defusion of the self-destructive death instinct in Anne's contemplated suicide. The aggressiveness Anne so crucially lacks is to be found in full measure in her daughter Nadine.

Nadine is sister to Xavière in *L'invitée*. Both girls are aggressive, truculent, belligerent, devious, malicious, at times self-deprecatory, and yet on occasion charmingly direct and open. 'It was true that Nadine, so concerned about her independence, so unreceptive to all criticism, to all advice, willingly spread out her life in broad daylight' (LM, p. 440: II, p. 64). And 'She was blind to a great many things, but she reacted strongly to those she did see – and without ever cheating' (LM, p. 104: I, p. 129).

Unlike Françoise and Xavière, Anne and Nadine are literally mother and daughter. Anne seeks to explain Nadine's aggressivity towards her in terms of a 'normal' mother/daughter rivalry for the father. Further, Anne suggests that Nadine has not proceeded normally through the Oedipus complex because she has failed to identify with her mother, to line up on the feminine side – Nadine as gender failure then: 'No little girl has ever fought more tenaciously to triumph over her rival for her father's heart. And she's never resigned herself to belonging to the same species as I' (LM, p. 82: I, p. 99).

The fascinating aspect of Nadine is her analysis of and resistance to a traditional construction of femininity. She is a gender guerrilla whose revolt spills over into an iconoclasm not unlike Xavière's. There seems to be a move within the text to contain Nadine's energy by explaining it away – either with reference to the Freudian scenario mentioned above or by suggesting that the root of the problem was that Anne had never wanted a child and had not loved Nadine enough, or that Nadine's behaviour is a consequence of the death of Diego, her lover. The reader has a further difficulty because Nadine is always presented from either Henri or Anne's point of view. I long to read Nadine's version.

Nadine fully understands women's position within patriarchy: she knows the score. In a nightclub with Henri, she ironically takes up the masculine position in relation to the strippers, discussing, connoisseur-like, the good and bad features of their bodies – 'Nadine silently examined the women with an expert, rather blasé look' (LM, p. 71: I, p. 86). Nadine mocks the cattle-market. She both recognises and trades on the exchange value of her body: '"How do you expect me to have affairs with men if I don't go to bed with them? Women bore me; I don't enjoy myself except with men. But if I want to go out with them, I have to sleep with them; I have no choice"' (LM, p. 463: II, p. 96). Nadine contrasts sharply with Josette, her contemporary. Both girls are caught up in the same economy – there is no mistaking the significance of the gesture made by Josette's mother as she hitches up her daughter's skirt to display the quality of the 'goods' (LM, p. 360: I, p. 449). Because Nadine is presented as physically unattractive, she is handicapped in the femininity stakes (Josette being a front-runner). On one occasion she tries to 'doll herself up' with grotesque results, 'her eyelashes looked like a sea urchin's spiny bristles and there were black smudges under her eyes' (LM, p. 165: I, p. 202). Usually, Nadine makes a point of not even trying to make herself look more attractive because she 'believed herself ugly, and it was out of spite, more than any-thing, that she disdained looking feminine' (LM, p. 461: II, p. 92, Anne's narrative). Nadine's different re-sponses to the traditional construction of femininity serve to point up its artifice, its status as construction.

The full subversiveness manifest in her rejection of this construction of femininity spills over into an unbrid-led attack on the value system of her parents and friends. In this she is very like Xavière. Talking to Henri

Simone de Beauvoir

about writers, she says, '"You're funny.... Worse than
a dope addict.... Dope addicts want to get everyone
else to take dope; you want everyone to start writing"'
(LM, p. 207: I, p. 254). Or later, '"How can anyone love
an intellectual? You have a set of scales where your
heart should be and a little brain at the tip of your
pecker.... Fundamentally ... you're all just a bunch of
fascists"' (LM, p. 211: I, p. 258). Unlike Henri and
Dubreuilh, she believes in direct action (hence her
involvement in acts of retribution against collaborators).
    For Nadine, life is a battleground. Toughness and
deviousness are the skills she brings to it. She can stir
up sympathy by making her nose bleed (LM, p. 471: II,
p. 106). She deliberately gets pregnant so as to trap
Henri: 'Henri was certain that, to force his hand, she
had manoeuvred her pregnancy by cheating on the
dates' (LM, p. 710: II, p. 431).
    Nadine is both tragic and courageous. She is caught
in a bind many women will recognise. As Anne puts it,
'"it's as a woman that she mistrusts herself. She needs
to be loved as a woman"' (LM, p. 466: II, p. 100). And
'"Nadine feels mutilated when she accepts her femininity
and also when she rejects it'" (LM, p. 467: II, p. 100).
Eschewing the friendship of women, Nadine desires
the company and camaraderie of men. Hence she steals
Lambert's motorbike which, for her is a 'symbol of virile
pleasures' (LM, p. 458: II, p. 88).
    The charm of Nadine is the robustness with which
she approaches life. What characterises her is her
aggressivity which is mostly, though not exclusively,
directed outwards. Her vulnerability shows through
when she is self-denigrating: '"No man would be ass
enough to marry me"' (LM, p. 270: I, p. 334); or '"I'm
rotten ... I'm always doing rotten things"' (LM, p. 747:
II, p. 479). If the text is taken as an enactment of the

112

drama of subjectivity (the drama not confined to a single protagonist), then Nadine represents the corollary of the narcissistic mode (Anne and Paule), that is, feelings of hate and aggression.

Anne, as the principal female protagonist, is the focus of the drama of the subject. The question is, how do the two dramas interact? Beauvoir simply wrote that Henri and Dubreuilh's 'point of view ... is that of action, finitude, life, is called into question by Anne in whom I have represented being, the absolute, death' (FC, p. 282: I, pp. 369–70). There is undoubtedly a tension, for the reader, between Anne's and Dubreuilh's perspectives, though I always have the feeling that Dubreuilh himself is quite impervious to Anne's interrogative stance. The issue of their different points of view is addressed in the text:

> 'Things are never as important as they seem; they change, they end, and above all, when all is said and done, everyone dies. That settles everything.'
> 'That's just a way of escaping from problems,' Robert said.
> I cut him off. 'Unless it's that problems are a way of escaping the truth. Of course,' I added, 'when you've decided that it's life that's real, the idea of death seems like escape. But conversely. . . .'
>
> (LM, p. 446: II, p. 72)

If Anne's question is what to do about death and Dubreuilh's is how to live in history, in time, we are faced with the need to relate death to history.

Norman Brown, in *Life Against Death*, discusses man, the neurotic animal, the maker of history. I shall try to use his ideas in order to place Anne's narrative within the dynamic of the text. In discussing Freud and death, Brown suggests that the world of man and the world of animals must be viewed separately. He asserts that it is a specifically human characteristic to repress the idea of death and to transform by that repression, what is at the animal level non-conflictual, that is, life and death unified, unopposed to one another. He argues that 'man's discontent implies the disruption of the balanced equilibrium between tension and release of tension which governs the activity of animals' (Brown, 1959, p. 90). He concludes that 'the disruption of the unity of Life and Death in man is to make man the historical animal' (Brown, p. 91).

Brown discusses Freud's statements on death and relates them to Hegel:

> Hegel was able to develop a philosophy of history only by making a fresh start and identifying man with death. And he develops the paradox that history is what man does with death, along lines almost identical with Freud's. Freud suggests that the aggression in human nature – the drive to master nature as well as the drive to master man – is the result of an extroversion of the death instinct, the desire to die being transformed into the desire to kill, destroy or dominate. Hegel postulates a transformation of the consciousness of death into a struggle to appropriate the life of another human being at the risk of one's own life: history as class struggle (the dialectic of Master and Slave, in Hegel's terminology) is based on an extroversion of death. And similarly Hegel's other fundamental category of history, human work or labor, is a transformation of the negativity or nothingness of death into the extroverted action of negating or changing nature. More generally, according to Hegel, time is what man makes out of death: the dialectic of history is the dialectic of time. . . .
>
> (Brown, p. 102)

For Brown, it is not the consciousness of death but its repression which projects man into history. Under the conditions of its repression, Brown suggests that the pleasure principle becomes the compulsion to repeat, which is manifested in man's striving to 'become' rather than to 'be', to progress, to seek after novelty. Anne's narrative is surely a comment on the public world of the history men. It represents what is hidden (repressed) there – death. It comes as no surprise to find the representation of that repressed 'with the women'.

The text does not divide tidily along a male/female line, with Henri representing the positive and Anne the negative, as was first suggested. Henri is a prey to many of the same questions as Anne. The difference between them is one of degree. Henri may indeed be a history man – but only just. That honour is reserved for Robert Dubreuilh, history man par excellence. The failure of the SRL, his new political party, is not enough to make him abandon his political project. He stands as the main locus of the masculine discourse within the text: Dubreuilh always knows, ' "Here in France we have a clear-cut objective" ' (LM, p. 148: I, p. 182); he knows the truth when he sees it. The reader never doubts his ability to answer the string of questions he sets himself:

> 'I'm writing a chapter on the idea of culture,' Dubreuilh said. 'What's the meaning behind the fact that man can't stop talking about himself? And what makes certain men decide they can speak in the name of others? In other words, what is an intellectual? Doesn't that decision make him a species apart? And in what measure is humanity able to recognise itself in the picture it paints of itself?'
> 'And what's your conclusion?' Henri asked. 'That literature still means something?'
> 'Of course.'
>
> (LM, pp. 300–1: I, p. 374)

Anne presents Dubreuilh as the agent of order and

meaning: 'From chaos, Robert had drawn a full, orderly world, cleansed by the future he was helping to produce' (LM, p. 61: I, pp. 72–3). On her return from the United States, Anne projects onto Dubreuilh the plenitude she so painfully lacks:

> on opening the door, I had seen him writing, head lowered, far away from me. How full that study was – that room in which there was no place for me! The air was saturated with smoke and work; an all-embracing mind summoned together here at will the past, the future, the whole world. Everything was here, nothing was missing.
> (LM, p. 647: II, p. 346)[7]

As Beauvoir herself put it, 'Dubreuilh occupies a key position in the book because it is in relation to him that Anne, his wife, and Henri, his friend, are defined' (FC, p. 277: I, p. 363). Dubreuilh is always sure of himself. His supremacy is never threatened because the space for the representation of self-doubt simply does not exist. In Beauvoir's words: 'his monologue remains a secret' (FC, p. 277: I, p. 363). Doubt, if doubt there be, is always Henri's or Anne's, projected onto Dubreuilh (as in the quotation above). I think that Dubreuilh is the real representative of the positive within the text, and not Henri.

My purpose in this reading of the text has been to locate the feminine, that is, the feminine defined as the site of resistance to the masculine. It is important to note that the feminine, in this sense, is not 'sex-bound'. Henri becomes the locus of the feminine when he perjures himself because he is then part of the resistance, albeit muted, to the determinateness of truth. Conversely, Anne is masculinised when she discusses the meaning of Henri's 'lettre de rupture' with Paule, because she is then on the side of unitary meaning. As I have already pointed out, the reader is never in any doubt as to what the truth is (Henri perjures himself and Paule is fooling herself). This is because the discourse of the text is masculine. To be on the feminine side, whether as reader or protagonist, is always to be in the weak position, to be marginalised.

The fact that the feminine discourse is to be found principally with the women represents women's position within patriarchy, their relation to phallic discourse. But that association between the feminine and the female renders the feminine perilously vulnerable to all the well-known strategies of 'put-down'. This is particularly true in Paule's case. It is Paule who most overtly problematises time in Chapter 1. ' "Do you think it's possible to bring back the past?"' (LM, p. 40: I, p. 47), she asks Anne, adding, significantly, that she must get Dubreuilh to tell her 'what time is'. But soon the text tips Paule's interrogative stance into a cover for her bad faith. Paule is condemned by Dubreuilh: ' "She wanted absolutely to make me say that time doesn't exist,"' and he adds, ' "The best part of her life is behind her and now that the war's over she's hoping to relive the past"' (LM, p. 50: I, p. 60). The feminine resistance to time so easily becomes a specifically female affair linked for Anne no less than for Paule, to unwanted wrinkles, the signs of physical ageing. The problematising of time is then reduced to the desire for sterile repetition (contrasting with the productive sort of the men) that is for a repetition of the same, no change, no progress.

The challenge must be to read beyond these marginalising strategies, to disentangle the feminine discourse which dramatises the dark side, the cost, of becoming a history man.

Notes

1. The published translation fails to emphasise Anne's function of *reducing* ('dulling, whittling away at, trimming') fears and anxieties.
2. The translation misses the point here. The contrast is not between Anne's state when she had not eaten but when she has not drunk. Thus 'sober' would be a better translation for 'in the morning before breakfast'.
3. 'Like' is, I think, too weak here. 'Love' would be better.
4. The original has no suggestion of Henri as 'father', rather he is in a less loaded sense the 'initiator of the message' which is then returned to him.
5. The translation fails to convey the ironic, 'you can't fool me' tone of Paule's responses. Hence 'Lucky you!' would be better than 'You're lucky' and 'Come off it!' for 'Please!' in the final utterance.
6. A literal translation of the final sentence would be 'I have lived with him as in myself, without distance.' In other words, Dubreuilh is part of Anne's self – their identities merged.
7. The original text uses the word 'plenitude' which is translated by 'how full' (second sentence).

Chapter Four

Les belles images: making silence speak

Female desire is courted with the promise of future perfection, by the lure of achieving ideals – ideal legs, ideal hair, ideal homes, ideal sponge cakes, ideal relationships. The ideals on offer don't actually exist except as the end product of photographic techniques or as elaborate fantasies.

(Rosalind Coward, *Female Desire*)

Twelve years separate *Les mandarins* and *Les belles images*, a novel no less rooted in its historical moment. Indeed, it might be said that the novel is 'about' the cultural climate of France in the mid-1960s. The 1960s, de Gaulle's decade, was a period in which French society felt the impact of a technological and consumerist culture which, since then, has become yet more powerful and pervasive.

The effects of this culture were considered particularly pernicious by those on the Left, who, according to John Ardagh, 'felt an embittered frustration at the rise

119

of a new way of progress that brushed aside their own theories and precepts' (Ardagh, 1982, p. 528).

Beauvoir expressed her hostility to this emergent society in *Tout compte fait* when writing about *Les belles images*, she said:

> I took up another project – the evocation of this techno-cratic society from which I keep as far away as possible, but in which, nevertheless, I live. I am hemmed in by it – through newspapers, magazines, advertising and radio . . . I wanted to 'bring out' what is today called its 'discourse'.
>
> (TCF, p. 137: p. 172)

Beauvoir's response was one of several, the most notable of which was probably Roland Barthes' (earlier) semiological analysis of popular culture in *Mythologies*, a series of essays written between 1954 and 1956. Barthes' raw material was the same as Beauvoir's (films, photographs, exhibitions, newspaper articles, advertisements). Barthes' analysis of these cultural phenomena aimed to show how a representation which was offered as 'natural', as somehow self-evidently and enduringly 'true', was in fact a construction in the service of bourgeois ideology. *Les belles images* is marked by this semiological project. When, for example, Laurence's husband sends her a bunch of roses after an argument:

> A ring at the bell: a bouquet of red roses with Jean-Charles' card: 'With love.' She took out the pins, undid the shiny paper: she felt like throwing them in the dustbin. A bouquet is always something more than mere flowers – it's friendship, it's hope, gratitude, happiness. Red roses – glowing love. And that was just what it was not. Not even sincere regret, she was sure of that: only a gesture towards the conventions of married life – no disagreements over Christmas.
>
> (BI, pp. 114–15: p. 136)

Using the language of semiology, we can say that the roses denote red flowers of a particular variety but that, within that society, they also convey or connote a particular message. Just as Laurence undoes the wrapping around the roses, so the text uncovers the signifying process. Laurence correctly decodes the conventional message and rejects it as a true statement. She then replaces it with her own interpretation of the gesture.

A representation of this meretricious, fashionable Parisian society is not new in Beauvoir's work. It exists on the margins of the intellectual milieu inhabited by the Dubreuilhs in *Les mandarins*. Anne and Robert, as influential intellectuals, constantly have to resist the blandishments of such personalities as Claudie Belzunce. Lucie Belhomme, mother of Josette, whom Anne meets at one of Claudie's salons, is a precursor of Dominique in *Les belles images*. Lucie owns *Amaryllis*, a successful fashion house. Devious, ruthless and hard-working, she plays the system and the field. In *Les belles images*, this sort of society takes centre-stage, is confronted head-on.

Why did Beauvoir, who found this society and its ethos so distasteful, devote an entire novel to exposing its shallowness and contradictions? (This question probably lies at the root of the suggestions that Beauvoir had written *à la* Sagan in this novel (Simon, 1980, p. 66).) Of course, this society was fair game, on the agenda for intellectuals. I want to suggest two other reasons for Beauvoir's representing it. Is it possible that this move to 'another scene' (the stylish world of advertising, overt image-construction) made it possible to confront and work through two particular problems: first the lures and impasses of the Imaginary, particularly as it relates to women; and second, the problem of representation in language (the literary work).

In the earlier chapters of this book, I have traced a recurrent and troubled preoccupation with the Imaginary (Françoise in *L'invitée*, Beauvoir in the autobiographies, and Anne in *Les mandarins*). What is repeatedly problematised is the question of female subjectivity. The engagement with this question tends to occur in private, in isolation from the social formation. In *Les belles images*, the impasses of the Imaginary are re-articulated, played out within the social formation, within ideology. The representation of the subject caught up in the Lacanian Imaginary is brought here into a relation with the subject in/of ideology. According to Coward and Ellis, 'Lacan's concept of the imaginary provides a route for understanding how the positioning of the subject in relation to language and, therefore, social relations is always accomplished in specific ideological formations'; the crucial point being that 'the subject in ideology has a consistency which rests on an imaginary identification of self' (Coward and Ellis, 1977, p. 76). This re-articulation of the Imaginary within the social formation dramatises the position(ing) of women within the dominant ideology in a particularly productive way. In *Les belles images*, the image is relentlessly shown to be a construct, whether it is an identity temporarily assumed by Dominique or an advert for a product. The test insists on the image as fictive, unsatisfactory if not downright deleterious to women.

Within the domain of advertising, distanced as it apparently is from the literary world, the issue of language and representation is implicitly addressed. The pivotal moment for this articulation comes when Laurence sits down, pen in hand, to write some advertising copy. It is surprising to see a Beauvoirian protagonist take up her pen for such a purpose. However, might the text not be saying something about the literary process as much as something about advertising? After all, the literary work, no less than advertising copy, draws on pre-existing codes in society in order to construct its world.

In Chapter 2, I touched on Beauvoir's difficulties with the relation between the literary product and reality. What Beauvoir desired was for writing accurately to represent and communicate *her* lived experience. She expressed regret and frustration when it seemed to her that the literary work had failed to achieve this, when, for example, readers 'misread'. In 'Mon expérience d'écrivain', a paper given at a conference in Japan in 1966, she said that for her 'one of the absolutely essential and irreplaceable tasks of literature is to help us communicate with each other' (E, p. 457). This view takes language as instrumental and not itself constitutive of a certain reality. It would be misleading to suggest that Beauvoir held a classical view of language and representation. The case is much more complex and confused. What is certain is Beauvoir's deeply critical attitude in the 1960s towards both the *nouveau roman* and the theories of the Tel Quel group. She asserted that for Tel Quel, a novel was 'a simple edifice of words in which nothing other than language itself is called into question and which means absolutely nothing' (E, p.449).

There is considerable evidence for suggesting that at this time, though still extremely influential, Beauvoir and Sartre were at odds with contemporary developments in literary theory, epistemology and psychoanalysis. In her biography of Sartre, Annie Cohen-Solal tells how, at a literary discussion in Paris in 1965 entitled 'Que peut la littérature', Sartre showed a lack of willingness to engage with the ideas of people such as Lévi-Strauss, Barthes, Lacan, Althusser and Foucault (Cohen-Solal, 1987, 574–5). It would be wrong to assume that Beauvoir reacted as Sartre did. There is, nevertheless, no doubt about her distaste for the avant-garde writing of the time.

The point I am trying to make about language and representation in relation to *Les belles images* is that, for Laurence, language/representation is radically adrift from the real world. Ideal images and identities are constructed in language which are anchored neither in the real world of hunger and deprivation nor in some essential human subject. To this extent, there is a recognition within the text of some of the insights of the intellectual movements of France in the 1960s, while at a different level in the text they are overtly criticised. For example, Laurence's husband, Jean Charles, is presented as a supporter of the 'new' theories:

> Jean-Charles and Dufrene were in agreement (they read the same periodicals): the idea of what constituted man was due to be overhauled and no doubt it would vanish; it was a nineteenth-century invention and now it was out of date. In every field – writing, music, painting, architecture – art was rejecting the humanism of earlier generations.
>
> (BI, p. 79: p. 94)

The strength of the text is that while there is here a critical attitude expressed (to Foucault's work), the text does not ultimately support the (retrograde) humanism of Laurence's father. It juxtaposes the two attitudes, problematises both without offering solutions.

Les belles images is marked by a significant shift in position compared to Beauvoir's earlier texts: it is not written predominantly from the masculine. It can be called a feminist text for two reasons. First, it is written from the feminine, that is, from a marginal place from which it seeks to resist the masculine hegemony (see

Introduction, page 8). As Beauvoir herself put it, the issue in this text was 'to make silence speak' (TCF, p. 137: p. 172). Laurence's achievement by the end of the novel is to have found the strength to say *out loud*, 'No!', that is, to *voice* her refusal of the coercive forces that surround her. This represents a radical departure from the earlier texts in which knowledge, certainty, are with the masculine, the phallic (Pierre in *L'invitée*, Sartre in the autobiographies, and Dubreuilh in *Les mandarins*). Up to this point, my strategy as reader has been to seek the often muted or hidden resistance to the masculine which, though suffering some attacks, tends to remain intact. All that changes in this novel because any notion of certainty, of fixed and unalterable truth, or indeed fixed identity, is refused. Second, the text is feminist because the feminine place is a woman's place, Laurence's place: the feminine and the female coincide here. Through Laurence's story, the question of female interpellation within ideology is addressed. The male protagonists are predictably complicit with the prevailing ideology. Unlike Laurence, they are blissfully unconcerned (and unaware), believing either in progress (Jean-Charles' optimism about the future) or in the 'old' values (Laurence's father's nostalgia for the past). The text does not present the prevailing ideology in terms of false consciousness, as if 'true' consciousness were a viable objective. This is my reading of the metaphor of the mole through which Laurence tries to make sense of her situation:

> She thought about a story she had read: a mole felt its way through its underground tunnels; it came out and sensed the clean fresh air; but it could not find out how to open its eyes. She told herself the story another way: the mole in its

underground dwelling found out how to open its eyes, and saw that everything was dark. None of it made sense.

(BI, p. 142: p. 169)

In the first version of the story we have a model of ideology as false consciousness because the mole could open its eyes and see the light. This version is rejected. Laurence does not see the light, find the answer (this is an interrogative text). In the second version, there is no light to be seen even if the eyes were open. This indicates that there is no 'outside' of ideology. The question for Laurence (and for us) is how to confront *that* knowledge.

The text offers a meditation on the image and in particular the ideal images offered to women in our society. As such, *Les belles images* is something of a pioneer text, one of many written by women in which an effort is made to understand how 'woman' is constructed in patriarchal society. I shall follow Laurence's progress as she recognises the process and then engages with her sense of dislocation, her ideological breakdown.

It was a stroke of genius to make Laurence an 'adwoman'. She understands the processes by which images (ideal homes, and so on) are constructed. She is somewhat distanced from them and therefore in a privileged position of knowledge in relation to them. This is not to say that she escapes the lure of the image. As Beauvoir put it, Laurence is 'sufficiently complicit with those around her so as not to judge them and honest enough to find this complicity a distressing experience' (TCF, p. 137: p. 172). Laurence is thus inside the prevailing ideology and distanced from it. Image-maker in the service of consumerism, Laurence sits down to write advertising copy knowing precisely what she is about: 'What a pretty advertisement this would make, what a pretty picture promising – for the advantage of some furniture-dealer, shirtmaker or florist – security, happiness' (BI, p. 18: pp. 20–1). Later, out Christmas shopping, Laurence and her husband buy a camera for their daughter:

> They bought a camera that was easy to work. There was a green signal to show when the light was right: if it was not, it turned red. Impossible to get it wrong. Catherine would be pleased. But it's something else that I should like to give her: security, a happy mind, the joy of being alive. I claim to be selling these things when I launch a product. All lies.
>
> (BI, p. 117: p. 139)

But this understanding of the process by which empty promises are made rebounds on Laurence so that she is forced to see herself as the victim as well as a manipulator of the system: 'You think you are very fond of a man: in fact you value a certain notion of yourself, an illusion of freedom or of the unforeseen – mirages. (Is that really true, or is it my job distorting my attitude?)' (BI, pp. 28–9: p. 33). When she is out shopping, we learn that 'because she loved these abodes of Paradise, carpeted with luxurious materials and planted with carbuncle-bearing trees that she had been able to talk about them right away. And now she was the victim of the slogans she herself had invented' (BI, p. 116: p. 138). Laurence's skill as an 'adwoman' is a curse equal to that of Midas: 'Everything she touched turned into a picture' (BI, p. 18: p. 21).[1] The connection between gold (money) and the image is surely not gratuitous.

It is Laurence's position as exploiter and exploited that lies at the root of her problem: she creates images and is one herself. It is the contradictions implicit in this situation which bring about the ideological and

127

psychological breakdown that ends finally in Laurence's retreat into illness. How does the text represent Laurence as a 'subject in crisis'?

She is figured as split subject at the level of narrative style. The text alternates, often abruptly, between a predominantly third-person narrative position (Laurence's point of view) and her first-person narrative position. This technique begins as early as the second page and is sustained throughout the text:

> Everything had been perfect, the sun and the wafting air, the barbecue, the thick steaks, the salad, the wine. Gilbert had told stories about travel and hunting in Kenya and then he had become absorbed in this Japanese puzzle – he still had six pieces to fit in – and Laurence had suggested an intelligence test, the one about the man who takes you over the frontier: it was a great success, for they had absolutely loved being astonished at themselves and laughing at one another. She had given out a great deal and that was why she was feeling depressed now: I'm a manic-depressive.
>
> (BI, pp. 7–8: p. 8)[2]

The reader has first to work out the relation between the two subject positions, that is, that Laurence occupies both. But the gap, the disjunction between the 'she-Laurence-in-the-world' and her subjective 'I' remains continually in play, a constant reminder of the cost of being a subject in and of language. This sustained interplay serves to destabilise any notion of a fixed identity and dramatises Laurence's precarious status.

The novel opens with a savagely satirical representation of Laurence's glossy magazine world. A smug, self-satisfied group of 'beautiful' people are enjoying an 'idyllic' Sunday in the 'ideal' country house owned by Laurence's mother. They are in temporary retreat from the pressure of life in Paris, which is presented as a merciless, pulsating power-house of productivity such that its inhabitants need sleeping pills, psychiatrists and gymnasium sessions in order to cope. The talk is of the latest exotic holiday destination, the latest audio equipment, cars and clothes. It is a society of excess. Laurence's husband's hobby is to collect useless objects. Gorged on the delights proffered by the consumer society, the group is presented as in no way unique. On the contrary, it resembles any number of other groups that also indulge in this (Imaginary) economy of the same, 'In another garden, wholly different and exactly the same, someone said . . .' (BI, p. 8: p. 9).

This is Laurence's world. However, although she inhabits a different milieu from her precursors in Beauvoir's texts, she has much the same problems. The sorts of metaphysical questions put by Françoise or Anne return here in a different, but for Laurence, entirely appropriate, form. Laurence repeatedly asks herself what everyone has got that she hasn't (BI, p. 13: p. 14: p. 17: p. 19: p. 71: p. 83: p. 126: p. 150), the question being posed in typically consumerist terms.

Just as Henri and Robert in *Les mandarins* 'get on with their lives' while Anne is stuck with metaphysical questions, so Laurence stands in a similar position in relation to her menfolk. Like Françoise in *L'invitée*, she is suffering from a sort of physical and emotional aridity, a mild form of aphanisis, loss of sexual desire. She recounts how, earlier in her marriage, 'for days and weeks on end I was not just a picture any more, but flesh and blood, longing and delight' (BI, p. 19: p. 22). In the early stages of her affair with Lucien, she says there was 'fire in my veins, the delicious liquefaction of my bones' (BI, p. 19: p. 22). But now Laurence and Jean-Charles' love-making is like everything else in her life – 'perfect' and yet unsatisfactory: 'After ten years of marriage, a perfect physical understanding. . . . Love too was smooth, hygienic and habitual' (BI, pp. 23–4: p. 27). As for adultery, Laurence concludes that the subterfuges involved are simply not worth it 'for these merely pleasant caresses, . . . for a pleasure so very like that which she had with Jean-Charles' (BI, p. 53: p. 63). So Laurence's extramarital relations lack spice – they too are banal, part of the routine of daily life.

This *taedium vitae* extends to all aspects of Laurence's life. When her father plays her a piece of classical music, she is unmoved: 'She did not listen. For a long while now music had no longer said anything to her' (BI, p. 31: p. 36). The music of Monteverdi or Beethoven has to do with an emotional intensity unknown to Laurence. All she has known is 'a piercing anguish now and then, a certain wretchedness of mind, forlornness, perturbation, emptiness, boredom – above all boredom' (BI, p. 31: p. 38). Laurence takes no pleasure in eating, being as indifferent to food as Jean-Charles (BI, p. 33: p. 38). Laurence quite literally does not desire anything (any object), either from her lover: ' "I don't feel strongly about things, you know. Advertising them has sickened me. . . ." ' (BI, p. 92: p. 109) or from her husband when they go Christmas shopping.

Not only does Laurence not desire anything or anybody, she is apathetic, she doesn't mind not minding; she no longer cries (BI, p. 22: p. 25). At a family party on New Year's Eve, she notes that she does not even wish (as she had the previous year) that she was somewhere else. She finds that she is unable to form an opinion whether it concerns liking or disliking a film (BI, p. 80: p. 95) or more complex issues of the day, such as feminism, psychoanalysis, the Common Market, or the 'force de frappe' (BI, p. 84: p. 99). Her conclusion is that really she has never made any decisions for herself, they were all made for her. She has just been proceeding down a pre-programmed track: 'I've always run along a set of rails. I've never decided anything; not even my marriage, nor my profession, nor my affair with Lucien – that came and went in spite of me' (BI, p. 100: p. 119).

Laurence comes to recognise herself as the subject/victim of ideological interpellation. The position available to her in society and which up to the present she has occupied, was, she realises, ready and waiting for her. The text dramatises that recognition and follows through its consequences. What enables this recognition is Laurence's understanding of the processes involved in marketing images. This has the effect of distancing her from the process of her own positioning (Laurence as image) and then throws it into crisis. This represents a threat to the system as well as to Laurence since the objective of ideological interpellation within capitalist society is to construct a self-determining, coherent individual who, being a necessary component in its functioning, will act appropriately within it. What we see in Laurence's case is a breakdown of that process so that she ceases to be able to act, to desire or say what she thinks. In society's terms, she needs to 'pull herself together'. She would then resume her functions of mother, lover, wife, consumer and producer of advertising images.

The text presents three ages of 'woman'. First, Catherine, Laurence's daughter, then Laurence herself, and finally Dominique, Laurence's mother.

Dominique is in her fifties, a tough, calculating and successful businesswoman. Laurence imagines someone summing up her mother: ' "Dominique Langlois? It was Gilbert Mortier who made her career." And that was unfair: she had got into radio by the side-door in '45 and she had succeeded by the sweat of her brow, working like a black and trampling over anyone who stood in her way' (BI, p. 8: p. 9). Like Juliette, in Angela Carter's analysis of Sade's heroine, Dominique is complicit with, works within, the phallic economy (to the extent of having prepared her daughter for the same sort of life). Although the implication that Dominique owes much of her success to the power and patronage of a man is rejected, what remains dramatically beyond doubt is her emotional dependence on him. Dominique is the highly vulnerable 'older woman' trying to keep her man, a man, who, though he is the same age as her, is attractive to younger women. Despite Dominique's success as a businesswoman, which has brought her economic independence, she goes to pieces at the prospect of losing Gilbert. As she says to Laurence, '"Socially, a woman is nothing without a man"', and, when Laurence points out that she has made a name for herself (surely a sign of having 'made it' in a phallocentric society), Dominique replies, '"Even if she has a name a woman without a man is a half-failure, a kind of derelict"' (BI, p. 120: pp. 142–3). For Laurence and her father, Dominique plays a succession of roles, adopts a variety of images: '"How is your mother?" "In great form." "Who is she copying at present?" . . . "I think . . . it's Jacqueline Verdelet. She has the same hair-do and she's abandoned Cardin for Balenciaga"' (BI, pp. 29–30: p. 34). Later, when Dominique has to face the fact that she is losing Gilbert, the play-acting has to stop. First, she loses her composure: 'Dominique wept. There was a flesh and blood woman with a heart under all those disguises, a woman who felt age coming on and who was terrified by loneliness: she whispered "A woman without a man is a woman entirely alone"' (BI, p. 97: p. 116). The loss of composure is rapidly followed by the emergence of a new Dominique, a vulgar, angry and vindictive woman: 'Laurence was dumbfounded by Dominique's sudden vulgarity. Never had she spoken in this voice, in this horrible way: it was some other woman speaking, not Dominique' (BI, p. 99: p. 117). Dominique's pitiable and all-too-familiar state stands as a warning of what Laurence's fate might be, were she to continue on the same track.

Then there is ten-year-old Catherine (whose reading includes that cautionary tale of the dangers of idealism, *Don Quixote*) who is not yet irrevocably embarked on the same well-trodden path as her mother and grandmother. While Laurence undoubtedly loves her daughter and is concerned about her future, she has an even deeper concern which derives from an identification with Catherine. When, for example, Laurence recalls the family discussing 'what to do about Catherine', 'she was overcome by a kind of shame, as though she had been Catherine and had overheard what they had said' (BI, p. 145: p. 173). This identificaton lends an additional urgency to Laurence's need to intervene in Catherine's case. Catherine's escape is to some extent Laurence's escape too.

Catherine, not yet fully drawn into the dominant ideology, has the 'pitiless gaze of children who are not playing at any sort of game at all' (BI, p. 25: p. 29).[3] She asks her mother one of the big Beauvoirian questions – Why are we here? (BI, p. 20: p. 23). What is more, Catherine is both aware of the misery that exists in the world and is deeply troubled by it. She recognises the injustice of the difference between the 'haves' and the 'have-nots'. Reality in the text, as opposed to the glamorous bubble inhabited by Laurence and company, is represented by the existence of misery and deprivation outside it and which it must marginalise.

Laurence has managed to avoid any contradiction between her life and that of the poverty-stricken by turning a blind eye to it. When she does pick up a copy of *Le Monde* in a conscience-stricken attempt to keep up-to-date (normally she relies on her husband to keep her informed!), she realises that she does not even have the necessary background knowledge to understand what she is reading and so she folds the paper up relieved because 'there was no telling what you might find in it' (BI, p. 38: p. 44). When Catherine confronts her with reality, Laurence first tries to gloss over her daugher's concern. She then sets about trying to discover the gap in the defences through which reality has gained access, intending to block it up.

The 'problem' is located in an image, a poster, 'The power of the image. "Two thirds of the world goes hungry," and that child's face, that beautiful face with its eyes too big and its mouth closed upon a terrible secret' (BI, p. 25: p. 29). This image, like the images of war and famine shown on television and in the press, are taken as 'true' representations of reality. There is a textual inconsistency here in that these images, unlike Laurence's advertising copy, escape analysis. The inevitable conclusion must be that the focus, the inter-rogation of the image in this text, is less concerned with the processes of representation than with a polemic directed against an emergent bourgeois consumerist society. There is here not only a textual blindness but also an irony since the reality which must be excluded from this 'beautiful' world constructed out of images returns to disturb it in the form of an image.

The need to 'save' Catherine is the catalyst which makes it imperative for Laurence to confront her situa-tion. The bind is that Laurence is very nearly the sort of person who is beyond doing anything to help her daughter. She is almost 'too far gone' to prevent her daughter from going down the same road as she has.

The issue centres on Catherine's friendship with Brigitte, a Jewish girl. Brigitte is badly dressed, though Laurence notes that with the necessary grooming and clothes, she would be pretty. Brigitte comes from a socially-aware family, the complete antithesis of Catherine's: her father is a doctor and Brigitte would like to study agriculture because, according to her grandfather, the future depends on such people. When Catherine receives a bad school report, Jean-Charles blames Brigitte's influence: ' "I wonder whether it's good for her to have a friend who's older than she is and a Jewess into the bargain" ' (BI, p. 110: p. 131). Catherine is despatched to a psychiatrist for assessment, who advises that the friendship between the girls should be gradually terminated.

The crisis comes when Catherine is invited to stay with Brigitte during the Easter holidays. During the family discussion about what should be done with her (Catherine being no more than an object (compare her with Xavière) in the family constellation is, of course, absent), Laurence must speak for her. So doing, she speaks for both herself and Catherine. She defends her daughter's right to Brigitte's friendship, invoking, in support of her argument, the distress she had suffered by not having been allowed the friends she wanted.

This spirited defence of Catherine's rights evokes an earlier exchange between Laurence and Jean-Charles when Laurence had been surprised at the violence of her opposition to the proposed controls on Catherine:

Follow your own little road without straying an inch; looking to the right or the left will be prosecuted; each age brings its own tasks; if you are overcome by anger drink a glass of water and do some exercises. It's worked for me, it's worked very well indeed; but nobody's to make me bring up Catherine in the same way.

(BI, p. 111: p. 132)

Laurence comes to realise that Jean-Charles' paternalistic attitude towards Catherine extends to her as well. When she had been upset after reading the story of a woman tortured to death, he had soothed her anxiety, treated her as a child and not taken her seriously:

Because of him she had calmed down and she had done her best to expel the memory, very nearly succeeding. It was mainly because of him that she had given up reading the papers from then onwards. And in fact he had not given a damn; he had said 'It's appalling' just to soothe her. . . . What a betrayal! So sure of his rights, so furious if we disturb the picture he has made of us, the exemplary little daughter and the exemplary young wife, and utterly indifferent to what we are in reality.

(BI, p. 112: p. 133)

The text here points to what feminists now recognise as a crucial problem for women in a patriarchal society. Laurence realises that the 'model wife image' is a specifically masculine construction, an image of 'woman' in which she fails to recognise herself and which she refuses.

Laurence turns to her father as a source of knowledge and advice. Some readers have taken his attitudes as representative of Beauvoir's own views. This is not surprising given Beauvour's no doubt well-known dislike for this society as well as the fact that in Beauvoir's earlier texts, a male protagonist has tended to occupy a more or less unassailable position of 'truth'. Until reading this text, I have tried to locate the feminine challenge to such superiorities. It is a subtlety of this novel that everything indicates that the position of 'truth' will lie with Laurence's father, representing as he does a countervailing value-system to that of Laurence's husband and associates, whereas ultimately this is not the case. Laurence's father offers a pseudo-solution, is a textual red herring.

Initially, the father is presented as 'wholesome', untouched by prevailing values, presumed to 'know', a moral being: '"I must be a hopeless old idealist – I've always tried to make my life coincide with my principles" "Personally I don't have any principles," said Laurence sadly' (BI, p. 30: p. 35). Father believes man has been 'crushed by technology'. He sings the praises of impoverished communities in Greece and Sardinia where 'the people did experience an austere happiness, because there certain values were maintained, the truly human values of dignity, brotherliness and generosity, which gave life a unique savour' (BI, pp. 71–2: p. 84). He is nostalgic, preferring the classic novel to modernist texts, Greek antiquities to abstract art. He believes in 'timeless' values and truths which exist outside the whim of fashion, which makes him a quintessential bourgeois. His response to the present situation is diametrically opposite to that of Jean-Charles and friends. However, he is like them in that he thinks he has the answers. For a long time, Laurence too thinks that daddy knows best. It is only towards the end of the novel, when she travels to Greece with her father, that his way is revealed as a dead-end.

The trip to Greece is a re-enactment of childhood, of learning from daddy. Knowledge of Greece comes to Laurence through the intermediary of her father, 'and Papa deciphering the letters written up over the buildings: way in, way out, post office. I liked gazing at that alphabet and rediscovering the childhood mystery of the language; and I was pleased that the meaning of words and things should come to me through him, as it had in former days' (BI, p. 130: p. 154). Laurence here is nostalgic for the Word of the father (Le Verbe), soon to be found inadequate.

In Greece, Laurence finds temporary respite from the alienating sense of herself as an image: 'I walked into an hotel bedroom . . . without having the feeling that I was playing the part of a tourist in a publicity film' (BI, p. 130: p. 155). Nevertheless, Laurence cannot suspend her critical analysis of the trip as product, packaged consumer goods. She finds that 'the Parthenon was just like one of those copies in false alabaster they sell in the souvenir shops' (BI, p. 130: p. 154). Here we see the power of the signifier (in this case the copy) such that the 'genuine article' (the Parthenon) is diminished by its fake. For Laurence, the tourists on the Acropolis have been conned by travel adverts: they would never admit to having been left cold by the Greek experience, 'They would urge their friends to go and see Athens and the sequence of lies would go on and on – in spite of all the disillusionments the pretty pictures would remain intact' (BI, p. 141: p. 168). Father too is contaminated by the economy of the image. He, no less than the tourists who endlessly photograph the ruins at Mycenae, is a collector of beautiful pictures, the only difference being that his are mental images stored away in his mind. Father's shop window is the museum case.

Finally, the Greek experience provides evidence to contradict father's notions about the nobility of communities living at subsistence level. Laurence becomes convinced, as she travels around the Peloponnese seeing the life endured by the people, that poverty is oppressive and ignoble. Father's discussion with a Greek they meet shows him both extremely well informed about political life in Greece and deeply cynical about the value of political intervention (BI, p. 139: p. 166). So daddy lets Laurence down and she has no alternative but to grow up.

Returning to France, Laurence has no sense of self, of herself as 'the young wife returning home': 'I was not a picture; but I was not anything else either: nothing.' (BI, p. 143: p. 170). It is in this diminished and vulnerable state that Laurence must confront her situation and the problem of Catherine.

Like Anne at the beginning of *Les mandarins*, Laurence's narrative of the Greek trip is produced retrospectively from the isolation of her (sick) bed. This narrative is interpolated into subsequent events.

Laurence's illness (anorexia) is triggered during the family meal during which Catherine's future is the main subject of discussion. Laurence finds herself totally outnumbered. No one else sees any objection to bringing Catherine's friendship with Brigitte to an end. The moment of crisis is reached when Laurence can no longer maintain her resistance to their plans:

> I felt my voice getting louder. Jean-Charles looked at me angrily. 'Listen, since Catherine agrees to go away with us without making a fuss about it, don't you go and make one.'
> 'She makes no fuss?'
> 'Absolutely none at all.'
> 'Well, then!'
> Both her father and Dominique said it together, this 'Well, then!' Hubert wagged his head with a knowing air. Laurence forced herself to eat but it was then that she had the first spasm. She knew she was beaten.
>
> (BI, p. 147: p. 175)

As Laurence imagines Catherine being taken to Rome

as planned, so her body speaks her refusal (Laurence as hysteric).

The news of the reconciliation between her father and Dominique and her failed attempt to make her father face the contradictions in his behaviour produce a further bout of illness. Laurence vomits after her dinner and retires to bed in a state of emotional chaos. Her feelings are described in terms of Malay krisses in a drawer. When the drawer is closed the krisses fight one another. However, when the drawer is opened, they are miraculously tidy, which is to say that society has Laurence neatly pigeon-holed. It is all quite simple: she is jealous of her mother because she has an incompletely resolved Oedipus complex (BI, p. 150: p. 179). Laurence rejects this explanation of her state. (This is reminiscent of Anne's rejection of psychoanalysis in Chapter 1 of *Les mandarins*; see p. 94.) It is from within Laurence's interior monologue (she is silent as far as the other protagonists are concerned) that she refuses this account of her state. This unspoken discourse is brought into confrontation with the normative psychoanalytical discourse purveyed by the opposition. The text presents the practice of psychoanalysis as a method of control, a way of bringing straying women back into line (onto the rails), a support to patriarchy.

There are further echoes of Anne in *Les mandarins* when, earlier, Laurence reflects on psychoanalysis and concludes that soothing away a patient's fears and anxieties leads to the dulling (a mutilation) of sensitivity and thus to abnormality (BI, p. 134: p. 159).

Jean-Charles' solution to Catherine and Laurence's problems is to despatch them to a psychiatrist. Laurence, like Anne before her, pushes beyond the meanings that this adaptive psychoanalysis would place on her. She locates the real problem in the deep disillusion she feels in relation to daddy who has let her down badly (BI, p. 151: p. 179). (I can hear some readers say at this point that Freud and daddy are one and the same oppressive person – but that would be to take a narrow view of Freud's theories and to ignore re-readings of Freud.) The turning point, Laurence's moment of triumph, comes when she refuses *vocally* to allow Catherine to be coerced, forced back onto the rails:

'No,' she cried aloud. 'Not Catherine. I shan't let what has been done to me be done to her. What have they made of me? This woman who loves no one, who is indifferent to the beauties of the world, who cannot even weep – this woman that I vomit forth.'

(BI, p. 152: pp. 180–1).

Significant also is Jean-Charles' reaction to this outburst:

In spite of herself Laurence's voice was rising; she talked on and on, she was not quite sure what she was saying but it did not matter – what did matter was to shout louder than Jean-Charles and all the others and to reduce them to silence. Her heart was beating furiously, her eyes blazed. 'I have taken my decisions, and I shall not yield.'

Jean-Charles seemed more and more taken aback; in a soothing tone he murmured, 'Why didn't you tell me all this before? It wasn't worth making yourself ill. I had no idea you took this business so much to heart.'

'To heart, yes; maybe I have no heart left, but this business – yes, I do take it to heart.' She looked him straight in the eye. He turned his head away. 'You ought to have spoken to me before.'

'Perhaps. In any case I have now.'

Jean-Charles is stubborn; but fundamentally, he doesn't take this friendship between Catherine and Brigitte very seriously – the whole thing is too childish to interest him much. And it was no fun, five years ago; he doesn't want me to crack again. If I stand firm I shall win.

(BI, pp. 152–3: p. 182)

Jean-Charles' opposition crumbles. Laurence calls the bluff of phallic power (it is, after all, a sham, a seeming value).

Les belles images is an interrogative and radical text. At the end, Laurence finds herself at the beginning. There are no easy answers here, no model women, no exemplary heroines (more 'belles images'?). If Laurence refuses the image/identity on offer, what or who is she? That precisely is the question that remains. The strength of the text is to have articulated that problem.

Notes

1. 'Picture' here translates the French 'image'. 'Image' should be retained in English on almost every occasion because of its place in the discourses of advertising and psychoanalysis.
2. I think the translation prejudges Laurence here: the original for 'manic-depressive' is simply 'cyclique' – she goes in cycles, up and then down.
3. This is not quite correct – Catherine is refusing to play the game, which I read as the adult game in which Laurence is caught.

The works of Simone de Beauvoir

The principal works of Simone de Beauvoir are listed below, the first date given is that of first publication in France. Details of an English translation (where appropriate) follow (the date given is not necessarily the date the first translation appeared).

Many shorter pieces by Beauvoir plus a wealth of biographical and bibliographical information are to be found in *Les écrits de Simone de Beauvoir*, by Claude Francis and Fernande Gontier (Paris, Gallimard, 1979).

1943　*L'invitée*, Paris, Gallimard
　　　She Came to Stay, London, Fontana, 1975
1944　*Pyrrhus et Cinéas*, Paris, Gallimard
1945　*Les Bouches inutiles*, Paris, Gallimard
1946　*Tous les hommes sont mortels*, Paris, Gallimard
　　　All Men Are Mortal, Cleveland, World Publishing Co. 1955
1947　*Pour une morale de l'ambiguïté*, Paris, Gallimard
　　　The Ethics of Ambiguity, New York, Philosophical Library, 1948

Simone de Beauvoir

| 1948 | *L'Amérique au jour le jour*, Paris, Morihien |

1948   *L'Amérique au jour le jour*, Paris, Morihien
       America Day by Day, London, Duckworth, 1957
1948   *L'existentialisme et la sagesse des nations*, Paris,
       Nagel
1949   *Le deuxième sexe* (2 vols), Paris, Gallimard
       The Second Sex, translated by H. M. Parshley,
       Harmondsworth, Penguin, 1972.
1951–2 *Faut-il brûler Sade? Les Temps Modernes*
       Must We Burn de Sade? London, Peter Nevill,
       1953
1954   *Les Mandarins*, Paris, Gallimard
       The Mandarins, London, Fontana, 1960
1955   *Privilèges*, Paris, Gallimard
1957   *La Longue Marche*, Paris, Gallimard
       The Long March, London, André Deutsch, 1958
1958   *Mémoires d'une jeune fille rangée*, Paris, Gallimard
       Memoirs of a Dutiful Daughter, Harmondsworth,
       Penguin, 1963
1960   *La force de l'âge*, Paris, Gallimard
       The Prime of Life, Harmondsworth, Penguin,
       1965
1960   *Brigitte Bardot and the Lolita Syndrome*, London
       André Deutsch/Weidenfeld & Nicolson
1962   *Djamila Boupacha*, with Gisèle Halimi, Paris,
       Gallimard
1963   *La force des choses*, Paris, Gallimard
       Force of Circumstance, Harmondsworth, Pen-
       guin, 1968
1964   *Une mort très douce*, Paris, Gallimard
       A Very Easy Death, Harmondsworth, Penguin,
       1969
1965   *Que peut la littérature?* a symposium edited by
       Yves Buin, Paris, Union Générale d'Editions,
       coll. «L'Inédit» 10/18, No. 249
1966   *Les belles images*, Paris, Gallimard
       Les Belles Images, London, Fontana/Collins, 1969

The works of Simone de Beauvoir

1968   *La femme rompue*, Monologue, *L'age de discrétion*
        Paris, Gallimard *The Woman Destroyed*,
        London, Fontana/Collins, 1971
1970   *La Vieillesse*, Paris, Gallimard
        Old Age, London, André Deutsch/Weidenfeld
        & Nicolson, 1972.
1972   *Tout compte fait*, Paris, Gallimard
        All Said and Done, Harmondsworth, Penguin,
        1977
1979   *Quand prime le spirituel*, Paris, Gallimard
        When Things of the Spirit Come First, London,
        André Deutsch/Weidenfeld & Nicolson, 1982
1981   *La cérémonie des adieux* suivi de *Entretiens avec
        Jean-Paul Sartre* août–septembre 1974 (auto-
        biography and conversations), Paris, Gallimard
        Adieux – Farewell to Sartre, London, André
        Deutsch, 1984.

Select bibliography

English translations of extracts quoted in the text from books marked with an asterisk in this Bibliography are the author's own.

Albistur, Maïte, and Armogathe, Daniel, *Histoire du féminisme français*, 2 vols, Paris, des femmes, 1977.

Ardagh, John, *France in the 1980's*, London, Secker & Warburg, 1982.

*Audet, Jean-Raymond, *Simone de Beauvoir face à la Mort*, Lausanne, L'Age d'Homme, 1979.

*Audry, Colette, 'Portrait de l'écrivain jeune femme', *BIBLIO*, XXX, No. 9, 12 November 1962: 3–5.

Bair, Deirdre, 'In Memoriam', in *Simone de Beauvoir: Witness to a Century*, Yale French Studies 72, Yale, 1986: 211–15.

Bakhtin, Mikhail, *Problems of Dostoevsky's Poetics*, trans. R. W. Rotsel, Ann Arbor, Ardis, 1973.

Barthes, Roland, *Mythologies*, London, Paladin, 1973.

Barthes, Rolannd, *Image–Music–Text*, Stephen Heath (trans.), London, Fontana/Collins, 1977.

*Beauvoir, Hélène de, 'Simone ma soeur, par Hélène de Beauvoir', *Marie Claire*, août 1986: 61–8.

Belsey, Catherine, *Critical Practice*, London, Methuen, 1980.

Select bibliography

Benveniste, Emile, 'Language and Human Experience', *Diogène*, 51, 1966: 1–12.

Benveniste, Emile, *Problems in General Linguistics*, University of Miami Press, 1971.

Brooks, Peter, 'Freud's Masterplot', in *Literature and Psychoanalysis*, Yale French Studies 55/56, Yale, 1977: 280–300.

Brown, Norman O., *Life Against Death*, New York, Vintage Books, 1959.

Carter, Angela, *The Sadeian Woman*, London, Virago, 1979.

Carter, Angela, *The Passion of New Eve*, London, Virago, 1982.

Carter, Angela, 'The Intellectual's Darby and Joan', *New Society*, 28 January 1982: 156–7.

Cohen-Solal, Annie, *Sartre*, Paris, Gallimard, 1985, translated as *Sartre: A Life*, London, Heinemann, 1987.

Coward, Rosalind, *Female Desire: Women's Sexuality Today*, London, Paladin, 1984.

Coward, Rosalind and Ellis, John, *Language and Materialism*, London, Routledge & Kegan Paul, 1977.

Eagleton, Terry, *Literary Theory: An Introduction*, Oxford, Blackwell, 1983.

Evans, Mary, *Simone de Beauvoir*, London, Tavistock, 1985.

Felman, Shoshana, 'Women and Madness: The Critical Phallacy', *Diacritics*, Winter, 1975, pp. 2–10.

*Francis, Claude et Gontier, Fernande, *Simone de Beauvoir*, Paris, Perrin, 1985, translated as *Simone de Beauvoir: A Life . . . A Love Story*, London, Sidgwick & Jackson, 1987.

Freud, Sigmund, *Civilisation and Its Discontents*, London, 1975.

Freud, Sigmund, 'Dora', in *Case Histories I*, Pelican Freud Library, 8, Harmondsworth, Penguin, 1971.

Freud, Sigmund, 'On Narcissism: an Introduction', in *Pelican Freud Library*, 11, Harmondsworth, Penguin, 1984.

Freud, Sigmund, *Beyond the Pleasure Principle*, in Pelican Freud Library, 11, Harmondsworth, Penguin, 1984.

Gerassi, John, 'Simone de Beauvoir, The Second Sex 25 Years Later', *Society*, 79–80, 1976 (Jan.–Feb.): 79–85.

Heath, Stephen, 'Difference', *Screen*, 19, 3, Autumn 1978: 51–112.

Heath, Stephen, 'Male Feminism', *Dalhousie Review*, 64, 1984: 270–301.

Simone de Beauvoir

Kojève, Alexandre, *Introduction to the Reading of Hegel*, Ithaca and London, Cornell University Press, 1980.

Kristeva, Julia, 'My Memory's Hyperbole', in *The Female Autograph*, Domna C. Stanton (ed.), New York, New York Literary Forum, 1984.

Kristeva, Julia, *The Kristeva Reader*, Toril Moi (ed.), Oxford, Blackwell, 1986.

Lacan, Jacques, *Ecrits: A Selection*, translated by Alan Sheridan, London, Tavistock, 1977.

Lacan, Jacques, *Encore*: Le séminaire XX, 1972–3, Paris, Seuil, 1975.

Laplanche, Jean and Pontalis, J.-B., *The Language of Psychoanalysis*, London, 1980.

Leclaire, Serge, 'Sexuality: A Fact of Discourse', An Interview with Hélène Klibbe, in *Homosexualities and French Literature: Cultural Context Critical Texts*, Stambolian, George and Marks, Elaine (eds), Ithaca and London, Cornell University Press, 1979: 42–55.

Lefort, Gérard, 'La dame au turban', *Libération*, 15 avril 1986: 11.

Lemaire, Anika, *Jacques Lacan*, London Routledge & Kegan Paul, 1977.

MacKeefe, Deborah, 'Zaza Mabille: Mission and Motive in Simone de Beauvoir's *Memoires*', *Contemporary Literature*, Vol. 24, Summer 1983, 204–21.

Marks, Elaine, *Simone de Beauvoir: Encounters with Death*, New Brunswick, Rutgers, 1973.

Marks, Elaine and Courtivron, Isabelle de, *New French Feminisms*, Brighton, Harvester Press, 1981.

*Memmi, Albert, *L'homme dominé*, Paris, Gallimard, 1968.

Moi, Toril, 'Jealousy and Sexual Difference', *Feminist Review*, No. 11, June 1982: 53–68.

Moi, Toril, *Sexual/Textual Politics: Feminist Literary Theory*, London and New York, Methuen, 1985.

Okely, Judith, *Simone de Beauvoir*, London, Virago, 1986.

Rolo, Charles, 'Reader's Choice', *The Atlantic*, June 1956: 74–81.

Rose, Jacqueline, 'Introduction II', in *Feminine Sexuality. Jacques Lacan and the Ecole Freudienne*, Juliet Mitchell and Jacqueline Rose (eds), London, Macmillan, 1982: 27–57.

Rose, Jacqueline, *Sexuality in the Field of Vision*, London, Verso, 1986.

Select bibliography

*Sartre, Jean-Paul, *Les carnets de la drôle de guerre*, Paris, Gallimard, 1983.

*Sartre, Jean-Paul, *Lettres au Castor et à quelques autres*, 2 vols, Paris, Gallimard, 1983.

Sartre Jean-Paul, *L'âge de raison*, Paris, Gallimard, 1945.

Schwarzer, Alice, *Simone de Beauvoir Today: Conversations 1972–1982*, London, Chatto & Windus/The Hogarth Press, 1984.

Simon, Pierre Henri, '"Les Belles Images" de Simone de Beauvoir', in Simone de Beauvoir, *Les belles images*, Blandine Stefanson (ed.), London, Heinemann, 1980: 65–9.

*Todd, Olivier, *Un fils rebelle*, Paris, Grasset, 1981.

Walters, Margaret, 'The Rights and Wrongs of Women: Mary Wollstonecraft, Harriet Martineau and Simone de Beauvoir', in *The Rights and Wrongs of Women*, Oakley, Ann and Mitchell, Juliet (eds), Harmondsworth, Penguin, 1976.

Wenzel, Hélène, V, (ed.), *Simone de Beauvoir: Witness to a Century*, Yale French Studies: 72, New Haven & London, 1986.

Whitmarsh, Anne, *Simone de Beauvoir and the Limits of Commitment*, Cambridge, Cambridge University Press, 1981.

Wilden, Anthony, *Speech and Language in Psychoanalysis*, Baltimore, Johns Hopkins, 1981.

Wilden, Anthony, *System and Structure*, London, Tavistock, 1980.

Index

Note: No entries have been made for texts by Beauvoir that are the subject of individual chapters.

Index

Brown, Norman O., 113

capitalist society, 131
carnets de la drôle de guerre, Les (Sartre), 18–19
Carter, Angela, 23, 47, 81, 132
castration complex, 23, 34
Civilisation and Its Discontents (Freud), 25
Cixous, Hélène, 16
closure, 57, 66
Cohen-Solal, Annie, 123
compulsion to repeat, 108, 115
consumer society, 119–21
contingence, 56
Coward, Rosalind, 119
Coward, Rosalind and Ellis, John, 122

death, 100, 106–7, 115
death instinct, 34, 107, 109
'death of the author', 55
desire, 26, 35
Dora, 23, 43
Dostoevsky, Fyodor, 90
dyad, 21
dyadic relation, 22, 27

Eagleton, Terry, 45
Ecrits (Lacan), 57
Encore XX (Lacan), 25
essence, 14
Evans, Mary, 24
existentialism, 5, 12, 14, 55, 93

family romance', 27, 42
Felman, Shoshana, 11
feminine, the, 8, 14, 31, 109, 116, 124

as meta-narrative, 59
as site of resistance, 13, 116, 124–5
femininity, 4, 9–12, 14, 19, 21, 23–4, 50, 110
for Beauvoir, 10, 73, 76, 79
Foucault, Michel, 123–4
Francis, Claude and Gontier, Fernande, 17–18, 48
Freud, Sigmund, 11, 22, 43, 113
Fort/Da game, 107
narcissism, 104
negation, 74

Gerassi, John, 3, 10

Heath, Stephen, 6–8, 16, 45
Hegel, Georg, 19, 33, 97, 109, 114
heterosexuality, 37, 42
Histoire du féminisme français (Albistur and Armogathe), 9
history, 113–18
homosexuality, 37
hysteric, 34, 140

'I' of the *énoncé*/of the *énonciation*, 53, 58, 63, 66–7
ideology, 122, 125–6, 131
identification, 26
identity, 4, 6, 11, 13, 21–2, 99, 104, 125
illness, retreat into, 37, 128
image, 71, 126, 134
Imaginary, 21, 26, 42–4, 82, 97, 108, 121–2, 129
incest taboo, 42
indirect free speech, 91
intersubjectivity, 26, 31

151